How I Sued PayPal and Won

By Paul Bezaire

Note for Librarians: A cataloguing record for this book is available from Library and Archives Canada at www.collectionscanada.ca/amicus/index-e.html
ISBN 1-4120-9432-1

Edited by Evelyn Alemanni
www.allea.com

1. Bezaire, Paul
2. Small claims court
3. PayPal

PUBLISHING™
Offices in Canada, USA, Ireland and UK

Book sales for North America and international:
Trafford Publishing, 6E–2333 Government St.,
Victoria, BC V8T 4P4 CANADA
phone 250 383 6864 (toll-free 1 888 232 4444)
fax 250 383 6804; email to orders@trafford.com
Book sales in Europe:
Trafford Publishing (UK) Limited, 9 Park End Street, 2nd Floor
Oxford, UK OX1 1HH UNITED KINGDOM
phone +44 (0)1865 722 113 (local rate 0845 230 9601)
facsimile +44 (0)1865 722 868; info.uk@trafford.com
Order online at:
trafford.com/06-1187

10   9   8   7   6   5   4   3   2

Dedication

This book is dedicated to all judicial officers, sitting in Small Claims Court, who see through the delaying tactics consistently practiced by defendants and make their decisions based upon the law and facts properly presented to them.

Other Writings by Paul Bezaire

The Man Who Sued God

The Cybernetic Athlete Golf Edition

The Cybernetic Athlete Bowling Edition

Pay No More Parking Tickets

The Rebel

Contents

Introduction..1

    How PayPal or eBay Makes Money with Your Money 4

Proceed with the Following Steps...8

    Send a Demand Letter...8

    File a Lawsuit Immediately...9

Case #1 10

PayPal Trick #1   Get the Court to Dismiss the Case 11

Case #2 14

PayPal Trick #2 Use Delay Tactics 14

    Timeline..14

Emails Trying to Delay Returning Funds 16

    Ready to Give Up 24

PayPal Trick #3 Try Intimidation 24

PayPal Trick #4 Be Less than Fully Open with the Court 27

PayPal Trick #5 Challenge Venue 30

PayPal's Motion Challenging Venue is Denied...31

PayPal Trick #6 If All Else Fails, Try..33

Insulting the Court 33

Judgment for Plaintiffs 35

Conclusion..36

Brief Folder 37

    Plaintiff's Claim 38

    Plaintiff's Brief 39

Appendix A 51

    Comb and Toher vs. PayPal, Inc. 51

    The Trial...68

    PayPal Trick #7 If All Else Fails, Try Deceiving the Court......83

    Declaration of Robert A. Pool 85

Appendix B 90

    Frequently Asked Questions...90

Appendix C 92

    The Court Grants Motion for Change of Venue and Dismisses
    Without Prejudice..92

INTRODUCTION

This book is not a substitute for an attorney. It cannot provide you with legal advice concerning your particular claim if you are wronged by anyone. Nor is it intended to encourage you to sue anyone. It is only to be used as a guide in the event you do want to sue in small claims court to get money owed to you. Because every situation is different, there is no way to guarantee that what is explained in this book will work for you. It has worked for me and others, so your chances are pretty good that it will also work for you.

Before you read any further I want you to know that I am not an attorney and do not intend to give you legal advice. (My attorney loves it when I put this in.) In this short document I will show you how PayPal has been successfully sued in small claims court. If you need further clarification of what to do, I suggest you contact an attorney.

JUDGES MAY FIND A SMALL CLAIMS CASE AGAINST COMPANIES LIKE PAYPAL OR EBAY DIFFICULT BECAUSE OF THE SMOKE AND MIRROR TRICKS USED BY THE DEFENDANTS. IN THIS BOOK, YOU'LL READ ABOUT SIX OF THE MOST-USED TRICKS AND HOW TO EXPOSE THEM. THIS BOOK CAN HELP BOTH PLAINTIFFS AND JUDGES UNDERSTAND THE TRICKS AND GET TO THE TRUTH.

In short, this is the process:

1. Determine if you have been wronged.
2. Send a demand letter.
3. File a small claims lawsuit.
4. Go to court.
5. Collect your money.

The following material walks you through the process.

There are only a few steps to take to file a small claims lawsuit.

1. **Determine if you have been wronged.** In Small Claims Court, you are not required to know legal theories—instead you simply state the facts of what happened. The judge will apply the law to the facts. So be prepared to explain only the facts of your case—how you feel you have been wronged.

2. **Send a demand letter.** See a sample demand letter below. Some states may require one before you can sue. Every jurisdiction is different but regardless of how long it's been since you have been wronged, *you might still be able to file your claim.* See also Email #4 in case #2 on p. 19 to see how the plaintiff demanded his money.

3. **File a small claims lawsuit.** Every jurisdiction has its own rules. Check with your local small claims court for help in filing. Check with your local courthouse to see where the small claims court is. You can also try going to this website to find the small claims court in each state. See Frequently Asked Questions in Appendix B.

http://www.consumeraffairs.com/consumerism/small_states.htm

4. **Go to court.** On the trial date, appear in court. The clerk may make a statement about waiving your right to a judge and having a lawyer authorized to hear small claims lawsuits hear your case. In my case below, I agreed to an attorney referred to as a judge pro tem. Be calm and simply explain your case.

Once you are in court, the heart of the whole controversy should come about at this time. The judge may start out saying that the court has received a letter challenging venue. (See below.) DO NOT interrupt as he/she speaks. Be calm. When he/she has finished you can tell the court that the venue is correct. You can say something like, *"Your honor, the venue is correct. A federal court found the user agreement and arbitration clause are substantively unconscionable under California law. The text of that whole case is in this book if you care to see it."*

If he is a good judge he will want to see it. You will hand it to the bailiff who will hand it to the judge. If PayPal shows up for trial to argue against you, DO NOT interrupt them. Always wait till they are finished and then speak.

5. **If successful in winning your case, collect your money.** I had no problem collecting my money from PayPal and neither should you. This is a subject not covered in this book. I suggest you type *small claims court* in Google. There you will find all kinds of help. For a small fee, you can have someone file your claim and collect your money. This may be the way you want to go if you have a doubts about what to do.

Most judges have never heard a case involving PayPal or eBay so it is not their fault if they decide the case in favor of PayPal or eBay instead of the person who lost money because of them, especially when they are not aware that a federal court had ruled in August 30, 2002, that the user agreement is *unenforceable*. Below are two cases you can read to get the feeling of what can happen. The first is a case where I was the first person to sue PayPal in small claims court and win. (Later, you will see many cases lost because I believe PayPal and/or eBay were less that fully honest with the court and the plaintiff did not know what to do to overcome that situation.)

Read the following cases carefully to get an understanding of how my nephew and I each won our separate cases. Understanding this will help build your confidence that YOU can also win.

Keep in mind that a magician uses smoke and mirror tricks to make a beautiful woman disappear. PayPal tried without success the same tricks to make this case disappear.

How PayPal or eBay Makes Money with Your Money

You might be interested to know why it takes so long to fight PayPal and eBay. Bernd Schneider is a great writer who has other articles about this subject at a great site called **AboutPayPal.org.**

http://www.aboutpaypal.org/how_paypal_makes_money_with_your_money

By Bernd Schneider

Alternative headline: How PayPal or eBay makes money with my money.

I have been using PayPal or eBay for a few months. Initially, I have been under the impression that their services would be free.

I don't mind paying for financial services. I don't believe in an economy in which things are gratis to consumers. That doesn't work. I want committed suppliers of services. They have to derive a benefit from providing a service. Otherwise, the quality of their services will decline, or will not be much to start with.

I furthermore believe that businesses providing a service ought to make a profit out of providing their service. I want to be tied into a healthy economic environment.

I believe that, in principle, a capitalist system provides a healthy economic environment.

They have tried the opposite in communist Russia. Ideologically, they were based on the idea that everybody works to the best of his capabilities, and draws benefit from the society to the extent of his needs.

This doesn't work by itself. It has to be enforced. People will search for loopholes. So it has to be enforced even stronger. People will still try to get an edge over other equals. So you need dictatorship.

The economic success of the US, and the bankruptcy of communist Russia are proof that a capitalist, profit-based economic order provides the healthier economic environment. Sure, capitalism needs to be regulated to prevent those who are

4

too smart to take undue advantage of those who have a harder time to compete. But this doesn't mean that the basic profit-based, capitalistic principle would be abandoned by regulating the conduct of competitors or businesses. Do we consent on this?

Now, here comes PayPal or eBay. Initially, so I (and many other people) had the impression, they offered something free. This did make me suspicious. Nobody can maintain a company and quality of service if everything is for free.

When I was told that I could pay charges, I immediately agreed. I am much happier when I know what a service costs. As long as I am told that it is free, I suspect that I will sooner or later be tricked.

Their charges were competitively priced, so I thought. I wasn't aware at that time that PayPal or eBay couldn't sustain their services on the charges they imposed.

Any business that loses money on the services they provide only has two solutions to its predicaments. One, they can find investors willing to provide more burn money (PayPal or eBay has been rather successful in this respect). Or, two, they can go for sideline businesses that do provide an income after all.

PayPal and eBay have found a way to do that, too.

When you engage in financial transactions using PayPal or eBay and channel money into their system, it will take a while until this money will again be out of their system, even if everything is conducted orderly.

But in practice, because of their habit of locking ("restricting") accounts and then requesting their clients to enter a time-consuming process of providing documentation, money often remains in their system for a considerable length of time. My own account of 467.11 US dollars has been "permanently locked."

The impression they'd like the public to have is that they restrict accounts to prevent fraud. But actually, they derive profit from restricting accounts, and from keeping them locked for as long as possible. And YOU have agreed to this by using their website.

Just read the following excerpt from their Terms of Use (downloaded December 14, 2001):

"PayPal or eBay will pool your funds together with funds from other Users, and will place those funds in accounts at one or more FDIC-insured banks ("Pooled Accounts"). You agree that any earnings on the Pooled Accounts will be the property of PayPal or eBay, and you will not receive interest or other earnings on the funds that PayPal or eBay handles as your agent."

So, they take your money, and my 467 dollars, and put it all together in an account, or several accounts, with proper banks, and pocket the interest. You, and I, get nothing.

And of course, as PayPal or eBay is facing economic problems, the incentive to make money simply by temporarily or permanently locking customer accounts, and then collecting interest on the withheld amounts, is a considerable factor.

I am surprised that they get away with this. No bank or other financial institution would.

Damien Cave, in his excellent February 23, 2001 article on PayPal or eBay, published by Salon.com, wrote:

"Its terms of use emphasize that PayPal or eBay is 'not a bank ... not subject to banking regulations.'"

The wording as quoted above seemed to reveal too blatantly their business strategy. The line "not subject to banking regulations" is no longer part of their Terms of Use.

Instead, on the version I downloaded on December 14, 2001, the section reads:

"PayPal or eBay is not a bank and the Service is a payment processing service rather than a banking service."

I don't think that their lawyers, or whoever drafts their legal documents, are very good with words, so they regularly have to rework their writings.

The form letter from them that provoked me to set up this site stated:

"Following an investigation, this account has been permanently locked due to violations of our Terms of Use. This decision may not be appealed."

I guess they'll change the above wording, too, though it may take a while. There must be more elegant, and more polite, methods to tell a customer that his 467 dollars have been virtually confiscated by a virtual bank.

Ups, no, they aren't a bank. They don't want to be one, either.

As Damien Cave reported in the above-quoted article: "…while the company considered buying a bank charter last year, executives ruled against it."

Why? Quote Peter Thiel, a co-founder of PayPal or eBay: *"The cost and regulatory burden was too high."*

Damien Cave: "The paperwork and all the restrictions of law were just too much."

Yeah, if PayPal or eBay were properly regulated, they couldn't just park my money indefinitely on their accounts, and pocket the interest.

Damien Cave quoted Peter Thiel with the following additional enlightening statement: *"Consumers didn't want another bank account, they want to move money."*

Yeah, I would like to move money, my money. For example, from PayPal or eBay's pooled account to my own account. For that purpose, I don't really care whether they call themselves a bank or a pen pal club.

I have lost 467.11 US dollars to PayPal or eBay's scheming. I will probably survive the loss of 467.11 US dollars. But, to be honest, I don't want PayPal or eBay to survive on the kind of schemes by which they got hold of those 467.11 US dollars of mine.

[Update: after several weeks, and after having found their attention with this website, they unrestricted my account, and I was able to withdraw my money. Please see the subscriber section for tips on how to make PayPal or eBay release funds, or write to me for individual advice.]

Proceed with the Following Steps

Since I know about their tactics, here's what I would do should I ever need to sue either PayPal or eBay.

Send a Demand Letter

I would immediately send them a letter demanding my money to be released to me within 15 days. I would explain why I believe they owe me money. I would tell why they owe me money in the same way I will tell the judge when I go to court. In the last sentence I would say: "I demand that you immediately release (*state the amount*) to me. If my funds are not received by (*state a date*) I will be left no choice but to bring legal action against you."

Below is a sample letter you can send while *substituting your own story of what happened to you.*

> PayPal
> 2211 North First Street
> San Jose, CA 95131
>
> (date)
>
> To whom it may concern,
>
> I recently sold an item on eBay (XBOX 360) for $300 and sent the package from Canada using a registered postal service. I got my money and the buyer got his Xbox 360.
>
> You held the funds and told me that you suspected fraudulent use on the buyer's end. I submitted all the required information and got an email back saying that the money was sent back to the buyer because the Canada post service I used did not provide sufficient proof of delivery, even though it says delivered on the website.
>
> I contacted the buyer and he said that he never filed a chargeback or reversed the transaction.
>
> I demand that you return my money by (date) or I will be left no choice but to file a small claims action against you.
>
> Signed,

File a Lawsuit Immediately

If they did not release my money by the date stated in my demand letter, I would not stand still for any of their delay tactics. I would immediately file a lawsuit against them in small claims court. Every state has different forms and procedures, so I would go to my local courthouse and check with the clerk on what to do. I could also type *small claims court* in Google or any search engine I was using. For a list of small claims courts in the various states, I would visit

http://www.consumeraffairs.com/consumerism/small_states.htm

If I preferred, and for a fee, I might look for a small claims services to file my case for me. By typing *small claims court* in Google, I would find many services that can do that for me.

PUNITIVE DAMAGES CAN BE AWARDED BY A COURT TO DETER SOMEONE FROM ENGAGING ANY FURTHER IN SUCH ACTIVITIES. ON PAGE 39 YOU WILL SEE WHERE DAVID REQUESTED THEM BUT BECAUSE HE DIDN'T ASK FOR THEM IN HIS ORIGINAL COMPLAINT, THE COURT DID NOT AWARD THEM. SO IF YOU SEEK PUNITIVE DAMAGES YOU BETTER ASK FOR THEM WHEN YOU FILE YOUR COMPLAINT.

Case #1

Now read about my case to see how I sued PayPal and won.

Having trouble with PayPal, I filed suit against them. I had purchased an item on eBay using the PayPal payment system. One of the reasons for using PayPal was to avail myself of their Money Back Guarantee to insure that the product I bought would be in good working order. When PayPal did not honor their Money Back Guarantee for the item, which turned out to be defective, I had no choice but to sue them in Small Claims Court for the amount of $150.00. (**Superior Court of California, West District, Case Number SM 04A01557**)

After being served with the Summons and Complaint, PayPal began firing all their guns at me. They began sending letters to the court challenging venue. They attempted to scare me into dismissing the lawsuit. One letter said in part, "If we do not hear from you, we intend to file a Motion to Compel Arbitration, along with a request that PayPal be reimbursed for its attorneys fees and costs associated with enforcing the terms of the User Agreement."

Another said that, "Plaintiff entered into a binding contract with PayPal according to which he agreed that for disputes of $10,000 or less, he would resolve the matter through binding arbitration or by filing a lawsuit in a court of competent jurisdiction in Santa Clara County, California."

I ignored that contention and filed my complaint in Los Angeles County. DO NOT let yourself be intimidated by either PayPal or eBay. If you have any questions about that you may want to talk to an attorney. (Years ago my rebellious nature was fueled by such scare tactics.)

Subsequently, PayPal again wrote to the court challenging venue. Were they not aware that the <u>Federal Court in Case C-02-1227 JF (Pvt)</u> in 2002 said the following with respect to the User Agreement? *"Having considered the terms of the User Agreement generally and the arbitration clause in particular, as well as the totality of the circumstances, the Court concludes that the User Agreement and arbitration clause are substantively unconscionable under California law and that arbitration cannot be compelled herein."*

PayPal Trick #1
Get the Court to Dismiss the Case

Read the following letter about how they tried to get the court to dismiss my case.

September 23, 2004
Superior Court of California
West District—Small Claims Division Santa Monica Courthouse
1725 Main Street
Santa Monica, CA 90401

Re: Challenge to Venue

Dear Clerk of the Court,

We are writing with regard to <u>Paul Bezaire v. PayPal. Inc.,</u> Case No. SM 04AO1557 currently scheduled for hearing on October 20, 2004 at 9:00 AM. Pursuant to Code of Civil Procedure Section 116.370, Plaintiff entered into a binding contract with PayPal or eBay according to which he agreed that for disputes of $10,000 or less, he would resolve the matter through binding arbitration or by filing a lawsuit in a court of competent jurisdiction in Santa Clara County, California. Arbitration may be conducted by telephone, on-line and/or based solely upon written submissions. A copy of the contract (User Agreement) is enclosed. The dispute resolution provision can be found at paragraph 15 of the Agreement.

PayPal or eBay respectfully requests that the court dismiss the pending action based on the agreement of the parties. If the court determines that this action was commenced in the proper venue, we request that the court postpone the hearing for at least 15 days as required by Code I Procedure Section 116.370(2).

Very truly yours,

(signed by Michelle Squires)

Michelle Squires,

Senior Litigation Paralegal

Their attempted defense to my filing a Small Claims action, in Los Angeles County, was based upon their contention that: "When he signed up for the account, Plaintiff agreed to the User Agreement for PayPal service specifically including the Legal Disputes section of the User Agreement" that said all law suits must be filed in Santa Clara, County, CA.

Why did they not also inform the court that a Federal Court had already found that their User Agreement was unconscionable under California law? (*My belief is that they were trying to trick the judge into believing that the User Agreement applies.*) Referring to the provisions of the User Agreement (Appendix A) the federal court said *"...these provisions made the User Agreement unconscionable, and appear to represent an attempt by PayPal to insulate itself contractually from any meaningful challenge to its alleged practices."* The Small Claims court awarded me judgment in the amount of $150.00 plus costs.

Trial was held on 10/20/2004. PayPal did not appear for the trial. It appeared that the expense of sending someone from San Jose to Los Angeles did not appeal to them.

On October 20, 2004, judgment was entered in my favor in the amount of $150.00 plus $52.00 costs to have them served and the filing of my complaint. (*The court will normally award you the cost of filing the complaint plus the cost of having them served with the Summons and Complaint.*)

While I am at it, let me give you the name of someone who served PayPal with my summons and complaint. I recently spoke with Jim who I found to be the least expensive process server for out-of-state service.

JIM SHEA INVESTIGATIONS
2924 David Avenue
San Jose, CA 95128
408-205-0548

Being dissatisfied with the judgment against them, PayPal filed a document requesting the court to Correct or Vacate the judgment which was eventually dismissed and reinstated by another judge.

Finally, I was insulted when PayPal sent me a seven-page confidential agreement to sign wherein they offered to pay me my $202.00 if I would sign the agreement. The agreement prohibited me from telling anyone about the terms of the agreement. They must have really thought I had mush for breakfast and was that stupid as to sign something that would prohibit me from sharing this information with other people who got stuck by PayPal or eBay.

Case #2
PayPal Trick #2 – Use Delay Tactics

This is a case you must follow to get the feeling of what happens in court. Understanding this will give you added confidence.

My nephew, David Bezaire, was in the middle of a dispute with PayPal who he claimed was holding, without reason, $1,400 dollars of his money. The first of 12 emails went back and forth between him and PayPal. (He did not find out how to sue them for his money until, by accident, he learned how I did it and won.)

Here's a timeline, followed by the related details.

TIMELINE

12/07/05	Case #05S01609 filed Heidi and David Bezaire v PayPal.
12/16/05	Proof of Service filed.
01/30 06	Court received letter from PayPal.
02/06/06	Case called. PayPal does not show up. Case continued to 03/06/06.
02/09/06	Clerk notifies defendant PayPal of continuance.
02/14/06	Letter re: change of venue from Bezaire placed in court file.
02/16/06	Case file sent to Division 1 for venue consideration.
02/17/06	Case returned to SC office. Date of 03/06/06 will stand.
02/28/06	Letter re: change of venue received from PayPal placed in file.

03/01/06	Case sent to Div. 1 for venue consideration.
03/02/06	Case called. Court rules hearing to remain for 03/06/06.
03/06/06	PayPal's motion on change of venue taken under submission.
03/06/06	Case called. Plaintiff and defendant present.
03/06/06	Plaintiff's Blue binder (p. 37) received into evidence.
03/06/06	Court takes matter under submission.
03/06/06	Parties to submit additional evidence by 04/07/06.
03/06/06	Matter continued to 04/07/06.
03/15/06	Clerk receives Pool Declaration (p. 85).
03/30/06	Exhibits placed in file for appearance on 04/07/06.
04/03/06	Letter from PayPal placed in file.
04/07/06	PayPal motion re: venue denied, (p. 31). Judgment for Plaintiffs.
04/07/06	Judgment for plaintiffs (p. 35) $1,434.00 + Costs $52.00. Total $1,486.00.

Emails Trying to Delay Returning Funds

Email #1 PayPal to David

On Oct 7, 2005, at 10:21 AM, service@paypal.com wrote:

Dear David Bezaire,

It has come to our attention that you may be the recipient of potentially unauthorized funds. We have initiated an investigation into this event. In the meantime, we have placed a temporary hold on the funds in question until the investigation is complete. This temporary hold will show as a deduction in your available balance. In the meantime, you are free to continue transacting using your PayPal account.

Transaction Date: Oct 5, 2005 21:06:05 PDT Transaction Amount: $1,434.00 USD

Pryor's Email: estates.collections@hotmail.com

If you have not delivered the goods or services related to this transaction, we ask that you delay or stop delivery until our investigation is complete as you may be liable for the amount in question. To assist us in our investigation and to determine if you qualify for the Seller Protection Program. Please send an email to pending-reversal@paypal.com with the following information:

1. The item, service or purpose of the purchase, and the associated value;

2. The name and address given to you by the sender (if an item was purchased);

3. If shipped, the company used for shipping, date of shipment and tracking number for the shipment;

4. Details of any other transactions related to the transaction(s) in question;

5. A phone number where you can be reached during the day and evening; and

6. Insurance information, if applicable.

Any additional information you have regarding this transaction, such as email correspondence, will further help us to expedite our investigation. Solving these cases helps us continue to offer PayPal as a secure and cost-effective payment service. We appreciate your cooperation and assistance.

Sincerely,

PayPal Account Review Team

Email #2 Response to email #1 October 7, 2005

The information below is in response to your request:

1. The item was 3, 1 ounce Krugerrand.

2. I was the sender. The name of the buyer was Greg Hewitt, 722 Station "H", Montreal ac h3g2m7.

3. It was shipped via US Postal Service, registered mail. #RR77971247705, October 6 2005.

4. None

5. *Phone number not shown here.*

6. The shipment was insured for the maximum allowed for registered mail of $1000.

I had an active auction for 2 krugerrands and the buyer asked if he could buy them now. I didn't have a buy it now price but offered to sell three additional krugerrands in another auction and include a buy it now price. I initiated the auction and he bought the three krugerrands. He did mention that he was going to have a co-worker pay for them and that she had a problem. Then I noticed that he had paid and I shipped the coins.

Thanks

Dave Bezaire

Email #3 Notification of reversal of funds

On Oct 16, 2005, at 7:34 PM, <u>pending-reversal@paypal.com</u> wrote:

Dear David Bezaire,

Thank you for contacting PayPal.

In accordance with PayPal's Seller Protection Policy, the following transaction(s) involving unauthorized funds have been reversed:

Transaction Date: Oct. 5, 2005 21:06:05 PST Transaction Amount: $1.434.00 USD

Buyer's Email: <u>estates.collections@hotmail.com</u>

The transaction(s) did not qualify for Seller Protection because:

The payment was not listed as "Seller Protection Policy Eligible" on the Transaction Details page.

Please note that this withholding is in accordance with our User Agreement.

In the future, you can protect yourself against fraudulent transactions by following the conditions of our Seller Protection Policy. For more information on our Seller Protection Policy in our User Agreement click

<u>https://www.paypal.com/sellerprotection</u> or copy and paste entire link into address bar.

If you have any further questions, please feel free to contact US again.

Sincerely, Lesley

PayPal Account Review Department PayPal. an eBay Company

Email #4 Response to email #3 October 17, 2005

PayPal,

What does this mean? Does this mean that I lose my $1410? As I wrote in my answers to your questions below, I already sent the item. When I tried to stop shipment on the package I was told that only law Enforcement could stop the shipment. Since PayPal discovered that fraud I thought that PayPal would be in the best position to get the shipment stopped. I called PayPal and asked for assistance in stopping the shipment and was told "We don't do that." You said that "We don't know if it is fraud." You knew enough to hold my money, you didn't know enough to help me hold the package? The package was delivered two days later. It seems unfair that I should bear the financial responsibility for this debacle. Firstly, Lucile Ent had her account used illegally. I am not sure how that is my responsibility. It is true that I shipped to an unverified address but when I asked PayPal to help stop the delivery, PayPal refused. It is because of PayPal that the person who committed fraud got away with it. You expect me to save you from fraud by not shipping to unverified addresses yet you refuse to prevent fraud by assisting me in stopping the shipment. How is that fair? I refuse to bear responsibility for this fraud. If PayPal had assisted me in stopping shipment of the package the fraud would not have been successful. I demand that PayPal reimburse me for $1410. Additionally, I recommend that PayPal bring criminal charges against the person that committed the fraud. If you are serious about stopping fraud, then act like it. Don't just leave your customers hanging and then take their money. It is a poor policy and needs to be changed. Thank you

David Bezaire

Email #5 Response to email #4

On Oct 20, 2005, at 10:35 AM, <u>pendingeversal@paypal.com</u> wrote:

Dear Heidi Bezaire,

Even though your transaction was not covered under our Seller Protection Policy. this does not stop you from seeking recovery for your lost funds. You can file a report with your local Police Department and follow this with a complaint to the Internet Fraud Complaint Center (IFCC).

The IFCC is partnership between the Federal Bureau of Investigation and the National White Collar Crime Center. The IFCC will review and evaluate complaints so that information can be referred to the appropriate local, state, or federal agency .Every complaint that is referred by the IFCC is sent to one or more law enforcement or regulatory agencies that have jurisdiction over the report. You can file a complaint with the IFCC at:

<u>http://www1.ifccfbi.gov/index.asp</u>

Sincerely, Candice

PayPal Account Review Department PayPal, an eBay Company

Email #6 Response to email #5 October 20, 2005

Candice,

Why is my transaction not covered by your seller protection policy? What did I do wrong? Also, how can you take my money without any explanation of why. What did the investigation find? Your communication is horrendous. If you take $1410 from me I want to know why. Dave

Email #7 *Response to email #6*

On Oct 24, 2005, at 2:12 PM, pending-reversal@paypal.com wrote:

Dear Heidi Bezaire,

Thank you for contacting PayPal.

If you would like to obtain specific account information for another customer, we would need to be presented with a legal subpoena by an attorney or a law enforcement officer. This individual only, may leave a message at (650) 864-8345 to proceed with this process once the subpoena has been obtained.

If you have any further questions, please feel free to contact us again.

Sincerely,

Christopher

PayPal Account Review Department PayPal, an eBay Company

Email #8 *Response to email #7 October 25, 2005*

I don't want any specific account information for another customer. Please read the following questions very carefully and answer them the best you can without providing specific account information.

1. Why was my transaction not covered by the seller protection policy?

2. Did the investigation find the payment was fraudulent?

3. If so, how did the fraud occur (in general terms)? Thank you.

David Bezaire

Email #9 Response to email #8

On Oct 28, 2005, at 3:34 AM, pending-reversal@paypal.com wrote:

Dear David Bezaire,

Thank you for contacting PayPal.

I apologize for the frustrations this has caused you. You received Funds that were reported to be potentially fraudulent. In other words, we have received notice that the holder of the originating account may not have made the transaction, be it from a credit card, bank, or PayPal account. As such, we had to return the funds to the party that had them taken from them without their authorization.

You are not protected from this reversal of funds under our Seller Protection Policy, as this transaction was not listed as eligible.

Please let me know if you need further assistance.

Sincerely, Katrin

PayPal Account Review Department PayPal, an eBay Company

Email #10 Response to email #9

October 28, 2005

Thanks for the info. I think we are getting closer to answering my question. Why wasn't my transaction listed as eligible?

Email #11 Response to email #10 November 2, 2005

Dear Heidi Bezaire,

Thank you for contacting PayPal. We apologize for the delay in responding to your service request.

Following the Seller Protection Policy is completely voluntary. However, if a seller chooses to engage in transactions not covered by the Seller Protection Policy. The seller assumes the risk associated with the transaction as well as any potential liability.

To learn the specific terms and conditions of the Seller Protection Policy, simply click on 'User Agreement' located at the bottom of any PayPal webpage. PayPal protects sellers from possible fraudulent payment activity by actively screening transactions for fraudulent buyers; from false buyer claims by providing a team of chargeback specialists and a resolution center that helps sellers resolve disputes in a fair manner; and by providing the Seller Protection Policy, which encourages good selling practices that in turn protect the seller from possible fraud.

Sincerely, Scott

PayPal Account Review Department PayPal, an eBay Company

Email #12 Response to email #11 November 2, 2005

I read the user agreement and the seller protection policy. I am still not sure why my transaction was not eligible by the seller protection policy. Can you please tell me the specific reason why my transaction was not eligible?

Ready to Give Up

David was at his wits end and ready to give up like most people probably do. Then, and by a stroke of luck, someone told him about my site at http://www.Rebel101.com where I have been telling people for a long time how I sued PayPal and won. When David called me, I advised him not to mess around emailing back and forth. They appear to use all this time to generate interest-free loans from people like him. Another reason is that when you give up, like he felt like doing, they have interest-free money for a very long time. I advised him to sue PayPal now and not fool around with them. Sending 12 emails over a period of 30 days is not good. So he filed in the small claims court in Bellflower, CA, case # LC05S01609.

PayPal Trick #3

Try Intimidation

Once the complaint was filed against PayPal, they became like a fish trying to shake loose from the fisherman's hook. They began by sending the following threatening form letter to David and his wife Heidi.

> January 27, 2006
> VIA FEDERAL EXPRESS
> Heidi and David Bezaire
>
> Re: Heidi Bezaire and David Bezaire v. PayPal. Inc. Case No.: LCOSSOl609
>
> Dear Mr. and Mrs. Bezaire
>
> We write concerning the lawsuit you filed against PayPal, Inc. in the Superior Court of California, County of Los Angeles, Southeast District, Small Claims Division. Specifically, we write to remind you that when you signed up for a PayPal account and agreed to the User Agreement for PayPal Service ("User Agreement") you agreed to specific procedures regarding disputes with PayPal.
>
> For disputes of $10,000 or less, you are required to resolve the matter through binding arbitration or by filing a lawsuit in a

court of competent jurisdiction in Santa Clara County, California Arbitration may be conducted by telephone, on-line and/or based solely upon written submissions A copy of the User Agreement is attached for your review The Legal Disputes provision can be found at paragraph 15.

In light of this agreement, we request that you dismiss your claim and pursue it either through arbitration or in the appropriate court in Santa Clara County. Please note that pursuant to the terms of the User Agreement, PayPal is entitled to seek its legal costs related to enforcing the dispute resolution provision if you refuse to comply with the terms of this section.

Please let us know by February 2, 2006 if you intend to withdraw the complaint currently pending in Bellflower, California. If we do not hear from you, we intend to file a Motion to Compel Arbitration, along with a request that PayPal be reimbursed for its fees and costs associated with enforcing the terms of the User Agreement.

If you have any questions, please feel free to contact me directly at (408) 967-1299

Very truly yours,

Michelle Squires

Senior Litigation Paralegal

Enclosure

CC: Superior Court of California County of Los Angeles Bellflower Courthouse Southeast District Attn: Court Clerk, Small Claims Division 10025 East Flower Street Bellflower, CA 90706

NOTE: Compare the text of the same letter they sent to me in Case #2 above. David told me that letter almost caused him to drop his lawsuit. The knowledge that this letter would probably be forthcoming gave him encouragement to hang in there.

In the introduction to my book The Rebel, I talk about how, as a young man, I responded to a similar trick of scaring an unknowledgeable person to fall for the tricks employed in the letter above. PayPal states "PayPal is entitled to seek its legal costs related to enforcing the dispute resolution provision if you refuse to comply with the terms of this section."

Now comes the point where I believe PayPal is less than honest with the court by sending it the following letter:

PayPal Trick #4
Be Less than Fully Open with the Court

January 27, 2006

VIA FEDERAL EXPRESS
Superior Court of California County of Los Angeles
Bellflower Courthouse -Southeast District.
Attn: Court Clerk, Small Claims Division
10025 East Flower Street
Bellflower, CA 90706

Re: Heidi Bezaire and David Bezaire v. PayPal, Inc. Case No.: LCOSSO1609

Dear Sir or Madam:

We write concerning the lawsuit Heidi and Dave Bezaire filed against PayPal, Inc. in the Superior Court of California, County of Los Angeles, Southeast District, Small Claims Division. Defendant PayPal, Inc. wishes to contest venue of the above-referenced Claim, scheduled to be heard on February 6, 2006 at 9:00 a.m. in Department 001.

When Plaintiff signed up for a PayPal account, he accepted the User Agreement for PayPal Service ("User Agreement," a copy of which is attached hereto). According to the Legal Disputes clause (Section 15 of the User Agreement), Plaintiff is required to resolve this matter through binding arbitration or by filing a lawsuit in a court of competent jurisdiction in Santa Clara County, California.

Furthermore, pursuant to the proper venue provisions outlined in Section 5(a)(1) and (2) of Plaintiff's Claim and Order to Appear, Plaintiff improperly filed his Claim in this court. Specifically, this courthouse does *not* cover the area where the Defendant PayPal is located and conducts business. Defendant PayPal is located in San Jose, California.

In light of Plaintiff s acceptance of the PayPal User Agreement, as well as the Court's proper venue guidelines, PayPal respectfully requests that Plaintiff dismiss his claim in the Superior Court of California, County of Los Angeles, and pursue it either through arbitration or in an appropriate court in Santa Clara County.

Please note that the disputes clause in the User Agreement used by PayPal and its parent corporation, eBay Inc., <u>has been routinely enforced by courts around the country, including the Superior Court of California, Counties of Los Angeles and Orange (see copies of Orders attached hereto).</u> Emphasis added; see Appendix C on p. 92.

In the event that the Court does not rule in PayPal's favor, we respectfully request permission to appear telephonically and that the hearing is continued for at least 15 days as required by Code of Civil Procedure Section 116.370(2). The Hearing in this matter is scheduled for February 6, 2006 at 9:00 a.m. PayPal is located in Northern California and will need to send a representative to Southern California on February 5, 2006 to appear in Court the following morning. PayPal's corporate travel department requires at least one week to arrange travel arrangements, including hotel accommodations and plane flight reservations.

Defendant PayPal has contacted Plaintiff and hopes to avoid continued litigation. In the event that settlement is not reached and PayPal is forced to appear in Court, PayPal fully intends to file a counter claim against Plaintiff in an effort to recoup the cost of being forced to send a representative to Southern California.

Finally, please note that Plaintiff served PayPal through our registered agent. For future correspondence pertaining to this case, I respectfully request that written correspondence be directed to me as follows:

Michelle Squires
PayPal, Inc. 2211 North First Street, San Jose, CA 95131

If you have any questions, please contact me directly at (408) 961-1299.

Very truly yours,

Michelle Squires, Senior Litigation Paralegal
Enclosures
CC (via Federal Express without enclosures):
Heidi and David Bezaire

NOTE: Please note that PayPal's statement that the courts have routinely enforced the User Agreement is a true statement. However, they fail to tell the court that in those cases, they had sent the same letter to the court and the court was not aware that a Federal Court had found that agreement to be substantively unconscionable under California law. In my opinion, this was less than fully honest with the court by implying that the User Agreement was still enforceable. I believe the court should, in these circumstances, impose sanctions on PayPal to deter them from this kind of activity. See a similar case on p. 31.

I want to applaud Commissioner EDWARD H. DRAYER sitting in the Superior Court, County of Los Angeles Southeast District, Bellflower Courthouse, Bellflower, California, who had the courage to study this case carefully and not fall for the deceits attempted to be perpetrated on his court. PayPal must have thought he had dog food for breakfast by sending him copies of ten Minute Orders and Clerks Notice of Ruling showing how cases against PayPal have, "been enforced by courts in this county, as well courts in the County of Los Angeles. On April 7, 2006, Commissioner Drayer ruled in David and Heidi's claim as shown in the following document.

PayPal Trick #5

Challenge Venue

By February 27, 2004 PayPal seemed to be fighting for their lives. They tried trick #5 by sending the following letter to the court again challenging venue.

February 27, 2006

VIA FEDERAL EXPRESS
Superior Court of California - County of Los Angeles
Bellflower Courthouse - Southeast District
Attn: Commissioner, Small Claims Division
10025 East Flower Street Bellflower, CA 90706

Re: Heidi Bezaire and David Bezaire v. PayPal. Inc. Case No.: LCOSSO1609

Dear Sir or Madam

We write in furtherance of our letter to the Court dated January 27, 2006 challenging venue of the above-referenced Claim and in reply to Plaintiffs' response dated February 10, 2006. This matter is scheduled to be heard on <u>March 6, 2006 at 9:30 a.m. in Department 001.</u>

Plaintiffs have indicated that they plan to proceed with the action improperly filed in Bellflower, CA. Further, Plaintiffs stated that they will be opposing PayPal's challenge to venue by relying on a 2002 federal court decision in which they claim that PayPal's arbitration clause was found to be "unconscionable." We take this opportunity to address the 2002 ruling and explain why it is unrelated to the case at bar, or the pending motion. Accordingly, PayPal's challenge to venue should be granted, and Plaintiff's claim should be dismissed.

If you have any questions, please contact me directly at (408) 967-1299.

Respectfully submitted,

Michelle Squires, Senior Litigation Paralegal

See denial of motion for change of venue on the next page.

PayPal's Motion Challenging Venue is Denied

SUPERIOR COURT OF CALIFORNIA,
COUNTY OF LOS ANGELES
SOUTHEAST DISTRICT, BELLFLOWER
COURTHOUSE, (-19466-)
10025 EAST FLOWER STREET, BELLFLOWER, CA 90706
TELEPHONE: (562) 804-8011

BEZAIRE, HEIDI v PAYPAL, INC.

CASE NUMBER: LC 05S01609*

MINUTE ORDER and CLERK'S NOTICE OF RULING

Court convened at 09:00 AM, on 04/07/2006;

in Division 001

Present: Honorable EDWARD H DRAYER,

COMMISSIONER, Judge/Comm. Presiding

J. Bowling, Deputy Clerk

and the following proceedings were had:

PLAINTIFF (s) BEZAIRE, HEIDI

(NOT) Appearing

DEFENDANT, PAYPAL, CHANGE OF VENUE IS REVIEWED IN CHAMBERS

DISPOSITION:
MOTION DENIED.

JUDGMENT ENTERED FORTHWITH.

Next came the trial. Don't let this scare you in any way. Everything is informal. But please, *never* interrupt the judge or anyone while they speak. Bring a stapler along should need to staple your lips together until the judge tells you that you can now remove the staples.

Before going to court, be prepared to present your side of the story carefully. Below is a Trial Brief David prepared. (A Trial Brief is not necessary but will be helpful in case you need to refer to anything.) He also presented a copy of it to the judge during his hearing. In that way the judge was able to review everything and help him come to a decision. A copy of David's Trial Brief is shown starting on p. 37.

In a separate document, judgment was entered as follows:

JUDGMENT AND
NOTICE OF ENTRY OF JUDGMENT

JUDGMENT WAS ENTERED AS STATED BELOW ON
(DATE): 04/07/2006

Defendant (name, if more than one):
PAYPAL, INC.

shall pay plaintiff (name, if more than one):
BEZAIRE, HEIDI,
BEZAIRE, DAVID

$ 1434.00 principal and $52.00 costs on plaintiff's claim.

PayPal Trick #6

If All Else Fails, Try Insulting the Court

In PayPal's letter to the court they state:

> "Please note that the forum selection clause in PayPal's user agreement and an identical provision in the user agreement of eBay Inc., (PayPal's parent company) has been enforced by courts in this county, as well courts in the County of Los Angeles (see copies of Orders attached to letter dated January 27, 2006)."

Did PayPal really believe that any knowledgeable judge would look at other Small Claims cases and find them to be controlling? Or were they saying, "Because other judges ruled in our favor, you should also." How about if they thought he was too stupid to fall for this trick? Let's look at what happened in just one of the cases they pulled off on a commissioner. (By the way, all information concerning plaintiff in those cases sent to the court was blacked out. I visited one of those courts to find out for myself what happened and why the plaintiffs lost.

In this case, the following letter was mailed to the court by eBay:

> November 29, 2004
>
> VIA FEDERAL EXPRESS
> Clerk of the Court
> Superior Court of California, County of Los Angeles, Western District;
> Small Claims Division
> 4130 Overland Avenue
> Culver City, CA 90231
>
> Re: Challenge to Venue. Case No: 04B01932
>
> Dear Clerk of the Court,
>
> We are writing with regard to Ellzev v. eBav Inc., Case No. 04B01932. Pursuant to Cal. Code of Civil Proc. Section 116.370, defendant eBay Inc. challenges venue in this action. Plaintiff entered into a binding contract with eBay under

which he agreed that for disputes of $10,000 or less, he would resolve the matter through binding arbitration or by filing a lawsuit in a court of competent jurisdiction in Santa Clara county, California. Arbitration may be conducted by telephone, on-line or upon written submissions. A copy of the contract (User Agreement) is enclosed. The dispute resolution provision can be found at paragraph 17(a) of the Agreement.

eBay respectfully requests that the court dismiss the pending action based on the agreement of the parties. If the court determines it wishes to hear argument on the venue issue, we request that the court postpone the hearing for at least 15 days as required by Cal. Code of Civil Proc. Section 116.370(2).

Very truly yours,

(signed)

Barbara Gooding

Paralegal Specialist, Litigation

*****

See the result of their case on the next page.

Judgment for Defendent

The Plaintiff lost because in my opinion, eBay was less than honest with the court. The letter dated November 29, 2004, is over two years after a federal court found the user agreement and arbitration clause substantively unconscionable under California law and that arbitration cannot be compelled. If the court had known about that case the result may have been different. So be prepared to point that case out to the court.

The ruling of the court is as follows:

CASE NUMBER: CC 04B01932

MINUTE ORDER and CLERK'S NOTICE OF RULING

The following proceedings were had:

PLAINTIFF(S) ELLZEY, MAX Appearing.

DEFENDANT(S) EBAY, INC. (NOT) Appearing.

NATURE OF PROCEEDINGS: CAUSE CALLED FOR HEARING RE:

CHALLENGE TO VENUE :

DISPOSITION: THE COURT RULES THAT THE VENUE IS IMPROPER IN THIS CASE AND ORDERS THE CASE DISMISSED WITHOUT PREJUDICE PER SECTION C.C.P. 116.370.

Conclusion

On my website, http://www.Rebel101.com, I receive a ton of mail from people who feel they have been wronged by PayPal or eBay and believe they are holding money that truly belongs to the letter writer. After going through what is sometimes a very lengthy explanation of why they believe PayPal or eBay owes them money, they ask for my advice. I explain that I am not an attorney, cannot offer legal advice, but do offer that any time I believe *anyone* owes me money I head straight for small claims court.

They tell me that PayPal or eBay's User Agreement says they must sue them in Santa Clara County, California and they cannot afford to sue them there. They tell me they cannot afford an attorney because their claim is very small. It's just not worth the effort. I hope this manual explaining how PayPal has been successfully sued in small claims court will give you needed hope and courage. (It doesn't really take much when you understand PayPal or eBay's tactics.)

To start, all you need is a firm belief that PayPal or eBay owes you money and you want it NOW. You can waste a lot of time writing them and hope they will release your money. Forget about the delay tactics. Send them a demand letter asking for your money. The longer they put you off the more interest they are getting on your money they are holding.

Now that you have an understanding of how to sue for your money in small claims court, read the following Trial Brief so you can see how my nephew David did it and so can you. Please write to me at Paul@Rebel101.com and let me know how you made out.

Brief Folder

A *Brief Folder* is used to brief the court on what happened, to show evidence, to show costs to bring this suit and is primarily prepared to present your case to the court. Although presenting a brief folder is not necessary, the judge will appreciate how thorough you are by making it simple for him to come to a just decision. You can offer the whole brief into evidence.

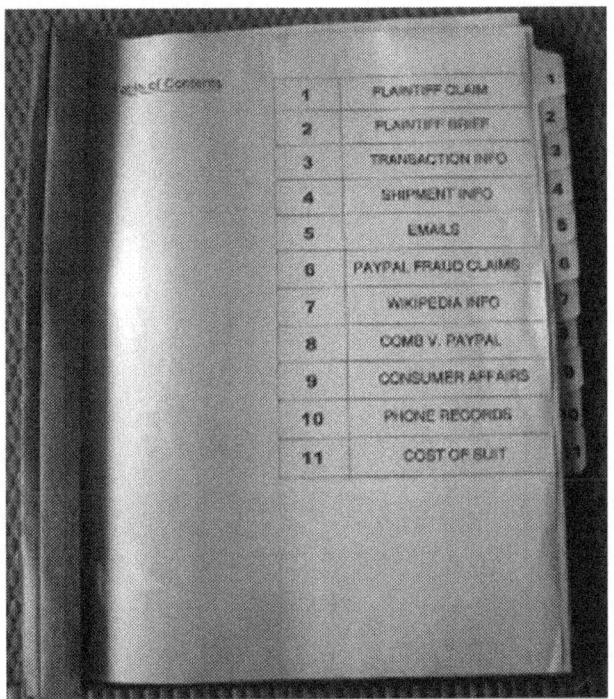

This chapter reviews all the items in the brief folder prepared for David's case.

#1 on the list is what you, the plaintiff, are claiming. Make it as simple as you can without throwing in so much information that it will confuse the judge. Here is David's claim. He might also use it to start his presentation to the court.

Plaintiff's Claim

The basis of our claim lies in the fact that PayPal advertises to be dedicated to stopping online fraud, and specifically to working closely with law enforcement to stop fraud. However, in our case when we requested that they contact law enforcement to stop a fraud that was in progress, PayPal refused.

Pay Pal's refusal to assist us in stopping the fraud allowed the fraud to be successful and resulted in us incurring a $1434 financial loss. Therefore, we are requesting a judgment against PayPal for $1434.

Additionally, PayPal has practiced unfair business practices for several years. PayPal has no incentive to change their business practices if they only have to return money they have unfairly taken. Therefore, we are also requesting punitive damages against PayPal in the amount of $3000 to help deter PayPal from practicing their egregious business practices.

If any part of this claim applies to you, feel free to use it.

#2 on the list is *Plaintiff's Brief.* This explains to the court in more detail what happened. It references other matters in the Brief. This Brief can also help the judge in the event he wants to read it later in chambers before making a decision. Again, stick to the facts.

Plaintiff's Brief

SUPERIOR COURT OF CALIFORNIA, COUNTY OF LOS ANGELES

Case No: LC 05SO1609

HEIDI BEZAIRE AND DAVID BEZAIRE ~ Plaintiffs

Vs.

PAYPAL, INC. Defendant.

PLAINTIFFS BRIEF Item #1

BACKGROUND

Pay Pal is an online payment company that offers its services to internet buyers and sellers to make and receive payments via the internet in a safe, speedy manner. A PayPal buyer sends money to PayPal and gives them shipping instructions. PayPal deposits the money into seller' s account and provides seller with the shipping instructions. Seller ships the item to buyer to complete the transaction.

On October 5, 2005, Plaintiffs auctioned three (3) Gold Krugerrand A Coins, online for $1,410 US to an online buyer via eBay. (See Item 3A Below.)

On October 5. 2005 Payment was made into Plaintiffs PayPal account. (See Item 3D)

On October 6, 2005, Via US registered mail, Plaintiffs shipped the Krugerrands to the buyer to address provided by PayPal. (See Item 4)

On October 7, 2005 Defendants notified Plaintiffs: "*It has come to our attention that you may be the recipient of potentially unauthorized funds. We have placed a temporary hold on the funds in question until the investigation is complete. This temporary hold will show as a deduction in your available balance.* " (See Item 5, email #1)

On October 11, 2005 Plaintiff called Canada Post who agreed to stop shipment. The last day, Canada Post said that only Law Enforcement could stop the shipment. (See Item 10.)

On October 12, 2005 Plaintiff called PayPal and asked them to help stop the shipment by contacting law enforcement. PayPal refused to assist Plaintiffs. (See Item 10.)

On October 13, 2005 the coins were delivered to buyer in Montreal. (See Item 4.)

On October 16, 2005, the transaction was reversed and $1,434 was removed from Plaintiff's PayPal account by PayPal with no explanation. Plaintiffs now have neither the purchase price nor the three Gold Krugerrands. (See Item 5, email #3.)

Review of the PayPal website implies that they are dedicated to preventing fraud and specifically that they work closely with law enforcement to prevent fraud. PayPal's representations on their website include the following:

1. PayPal's Fraud Investigation Team is highly experienced in fighting online fraud.

2. Several Members of the team are former law enforcement officials with extensive experience fighting online fraud.

3. PayPal's fraud investigation team focus on:
    1. Identifying and preventing fraud before it occurs.
    2. Detecting fraud in process.
    3. Mitigating loss if fraud does occur.
    4. Delivering information to law enforcement around the world to help stop those committing fraud
    5. Our dedicated fraud teams - in combination with our advanced technology - are here to help ensure your accounts remain safe from fraud.
    (See Item 6A -"PayPal We Work 24/7 to Protect You")

Elsewhere on their website Pay Pal represents:

•   Cooperation and shared investigations with FBI and other law enforcement agencies. (See Item 6B - "PayPal Protection for Sellers")

•   PayPal is also actively involved in working with law enforcement agencies to stop people who perpetrate online fraud and to reduce risk of other illegal activities.

- An experienced fraud prevention team including former law enforcement officials has helped protect the integrity of PayPal's transactions...

(See Item 6C - PayPal Fraud Protection)

The information on the PayPal website implies that they are expert at preventing fraud. They mention in several places that they specifically work with law enforcement to prevent fraud. In fact when asked to contact law enforcement to stop shipment of the coins, Pay pal refused. PayPal's refusal to contact law enforcement allowed the fraud to be successful.

PayPal reversed the transaction and took the money out of Plaintiff's with no explanation. PayPal claims that the buyer **may** have fraudulently made payment When plaintiffs asked PayPal what their investigation revealed PayPal replied *"If you would like to obtain specific account information for another customer we would need to be presented with a legal subpoena by an attorney or law enforcement officer ."* (See Item 5, Email # 6, 7, 8, 9)

Plaintiff's experience with PayPal is not an anomaly. PayPal has practiced unfair business practices for several years and continues to practice them. US District Court Case, Comb v PayPal states:

- Pay Pal has a backlog of over l00,000 unanswered customer complaints, a fact that has led the Better Business Bureau to revoke its seal of approval. (See Item 8.)

- The User Agreement for PayPal Services, which are the business practices under which PayPal operates was ruled to be *"substantively unconscionable under California law"* (See Item 8.)

- http://www.consumelafrails.com/online/paypal_02.html is a site with myriad unresolved complaints against PayPal filed by sellers. Some complaints are nearly identical to our case. (See Item 9.)

Due to the fact that in spite of claiming specifically to working with law enforcement to stop fraud, PayPal refused to do so when requested. This negligence allowed fraud to be successful resulting in a financial loss to plaintiffs. Also, to help deter PayPal from practicing unconscionable business practices, Plaintiffs request punitive damages. Plaintiffs ask for a judgment against PayPal as follows:

1. The sum of $1,434 for actual out of pocket loss;
2. Interest on the money withheld in the amount of $24, (5% for 4 months);
3. Costs of suit in the amount of $80;
4. Punitive damages in the amount of $3000.

Heidi Bezaire   David Bezaire   Dated

#3 in the list is the **Transaction Information. Item 3A** shows the listing on eBay of his three coins he was selling.

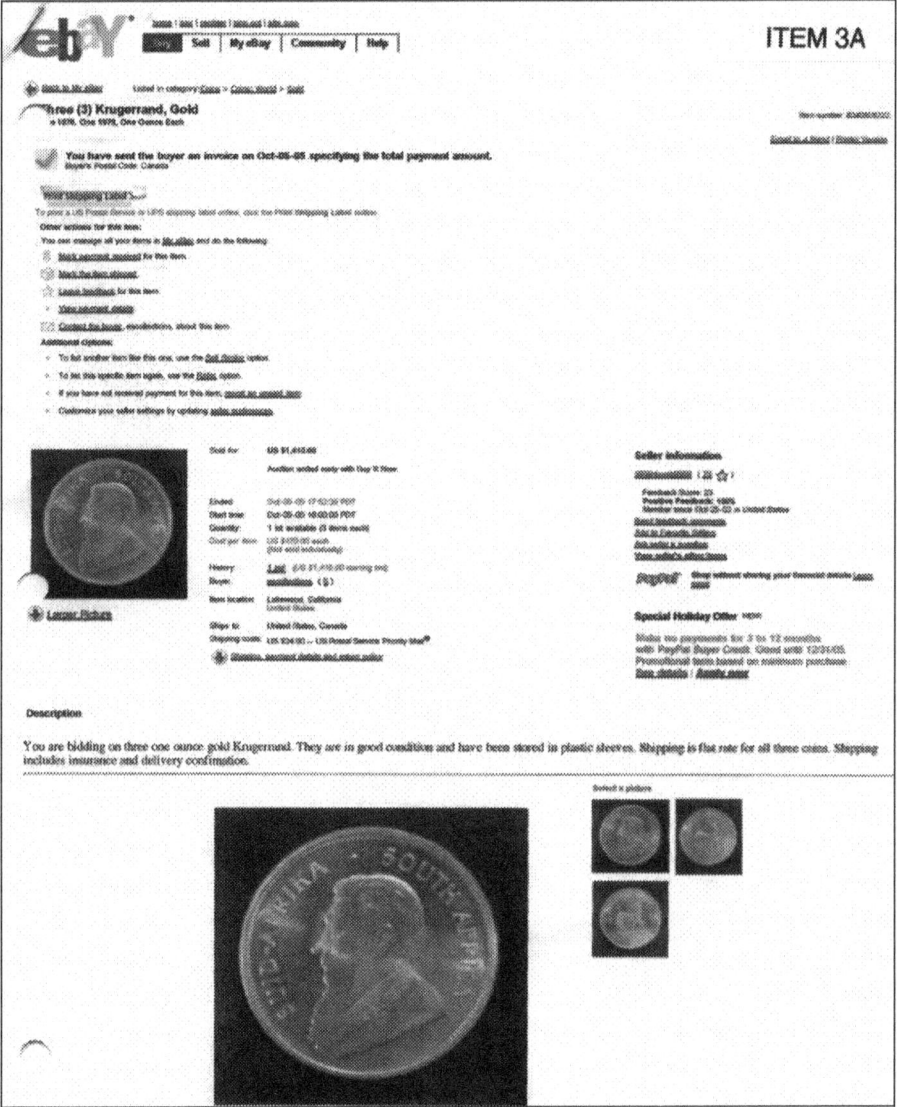

Item 3B shows he sold the coins.

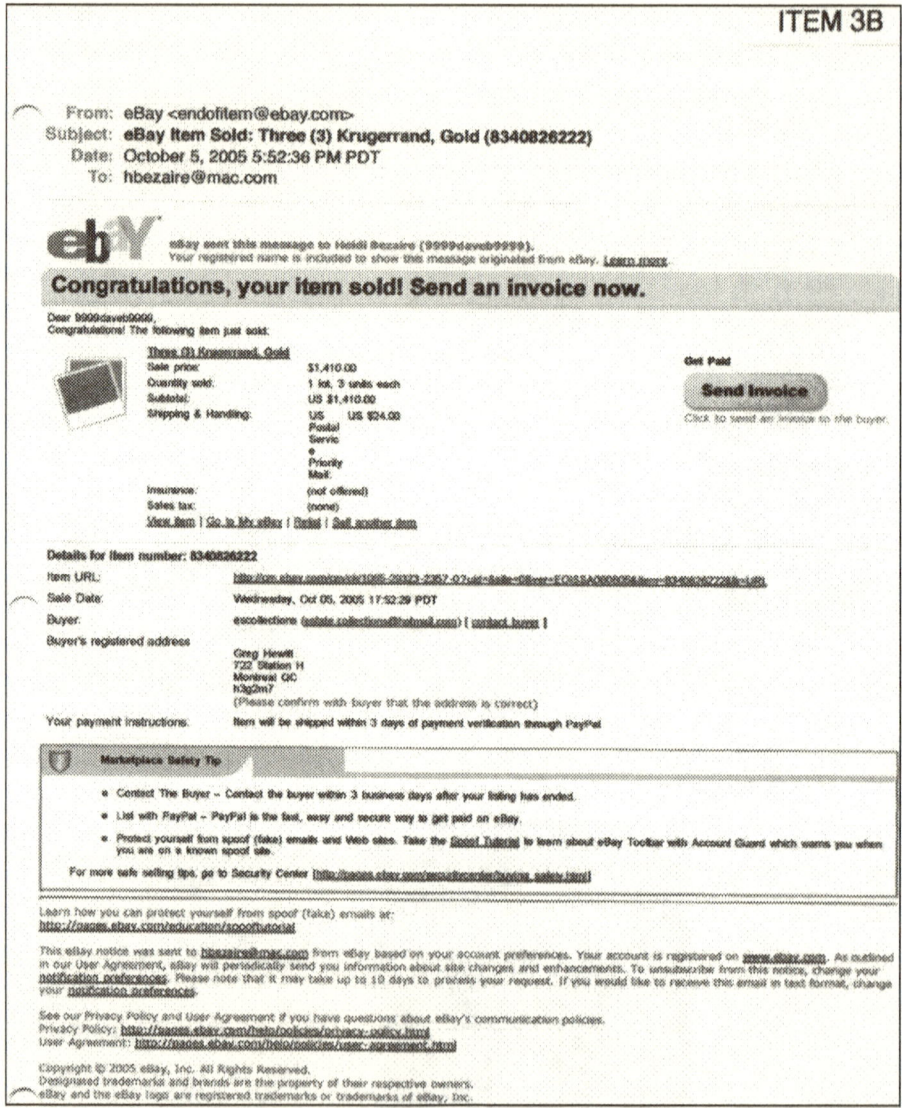

Item 3C shows payment by the buyer for the coins.

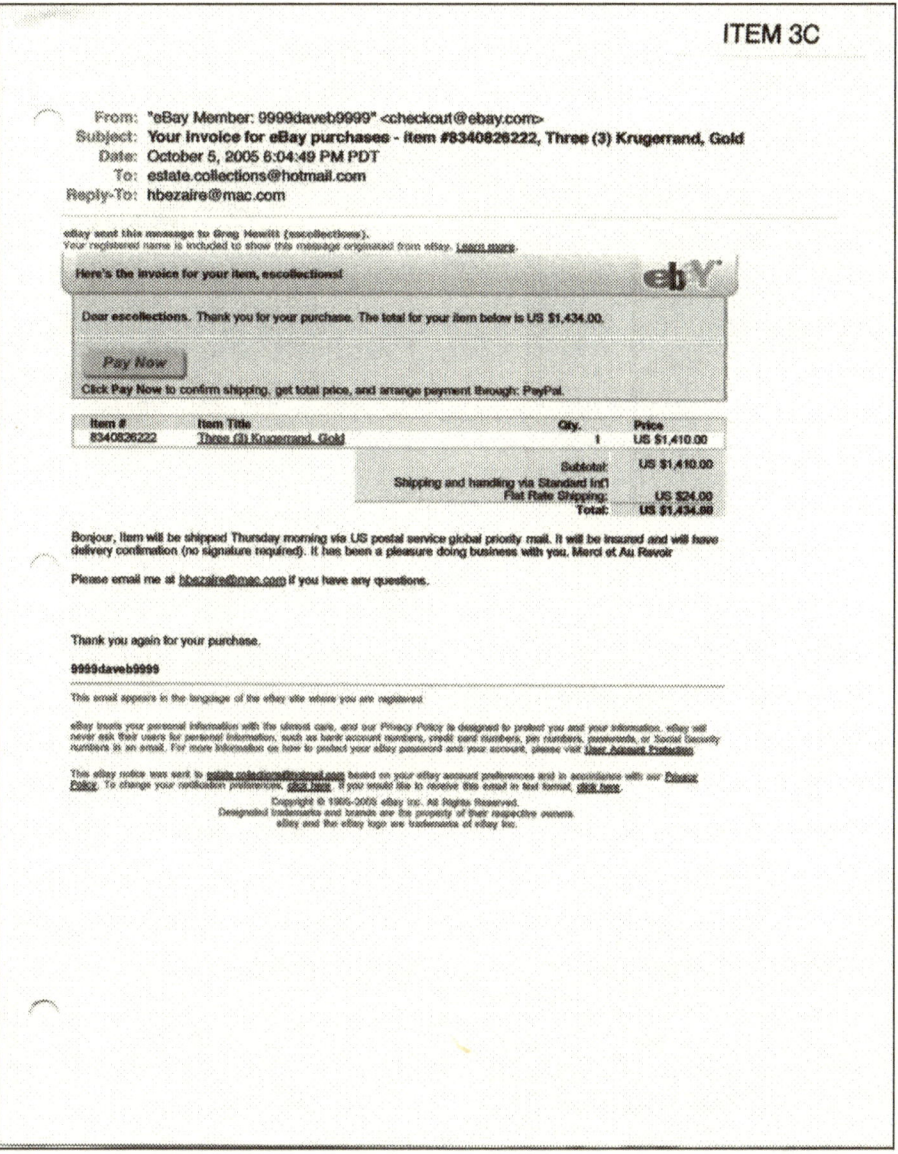

Item 3D shows David received an eBay Instant Payment of $1,434.00 from the buyer.

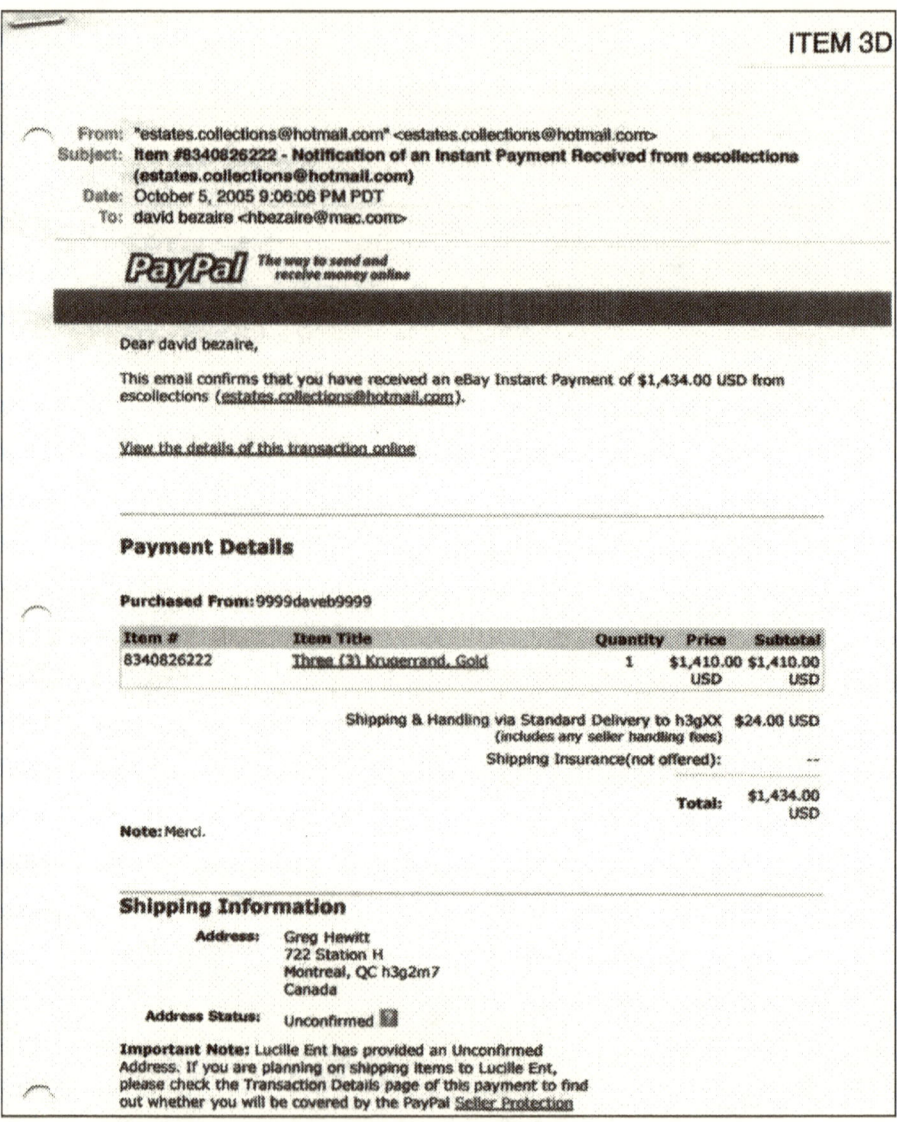

ITEM 3D

From: "estates.collections@hotmail.com" <estates.collections@hotmail.com>
Subject: Item #8340826222 - Notification of an Instant Payment Received from escollections (estates.collections@hotmail.com)
Date: October 5, 2005 9:06:06 PM PDT
To: david bezaire <hbezaire@mac.com>

PayPal *The way to send and receive money online*

Dear david bezaire,

This email confirms that you have received an eBay Instant Payment of **$1,434.00 USD** from escollections (estates.collections@hotmail.com).

View the details of this transaction online

Payment Details

Purchased From: 9999daveb9999

Item #	Item Title	Quantity	Price	Subtotal
8340826222	Three (3) Krugerrand, Gold	1	$1,410.00 USD	$1,410.00 USD

Shipping & Handling via Standard Delivery to h3gXX $24.00 USD
(includes any seller handling fees)
Shipping Insurance(not offered): --

Total: $1,434.00 USD

Note: Merci.

Shipping Information

Address: Greg Hewitt
722 Station H
Montreal, QC h3g2m7
Canada

Address Status: Unconfirmed

Important Note: Lucille Ent has provided an Unconfirmed Address. If you are planning on shipping items to Lucille Ent, please check the Transaction Details page of this payment to find out whether you will be covered by the PayPal Seller Protection

Item 3E shows a Reversal of Payment to David's account.

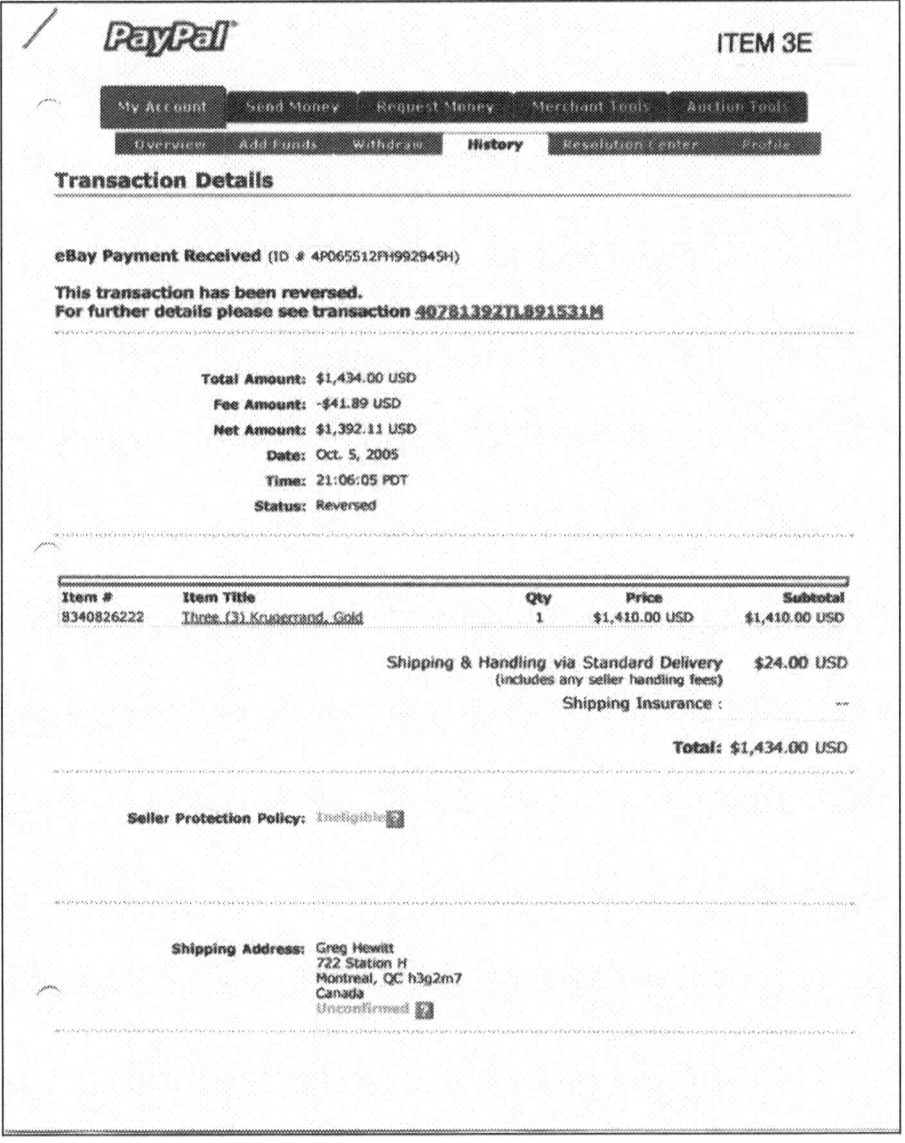

#4 shows the Shipment Information.

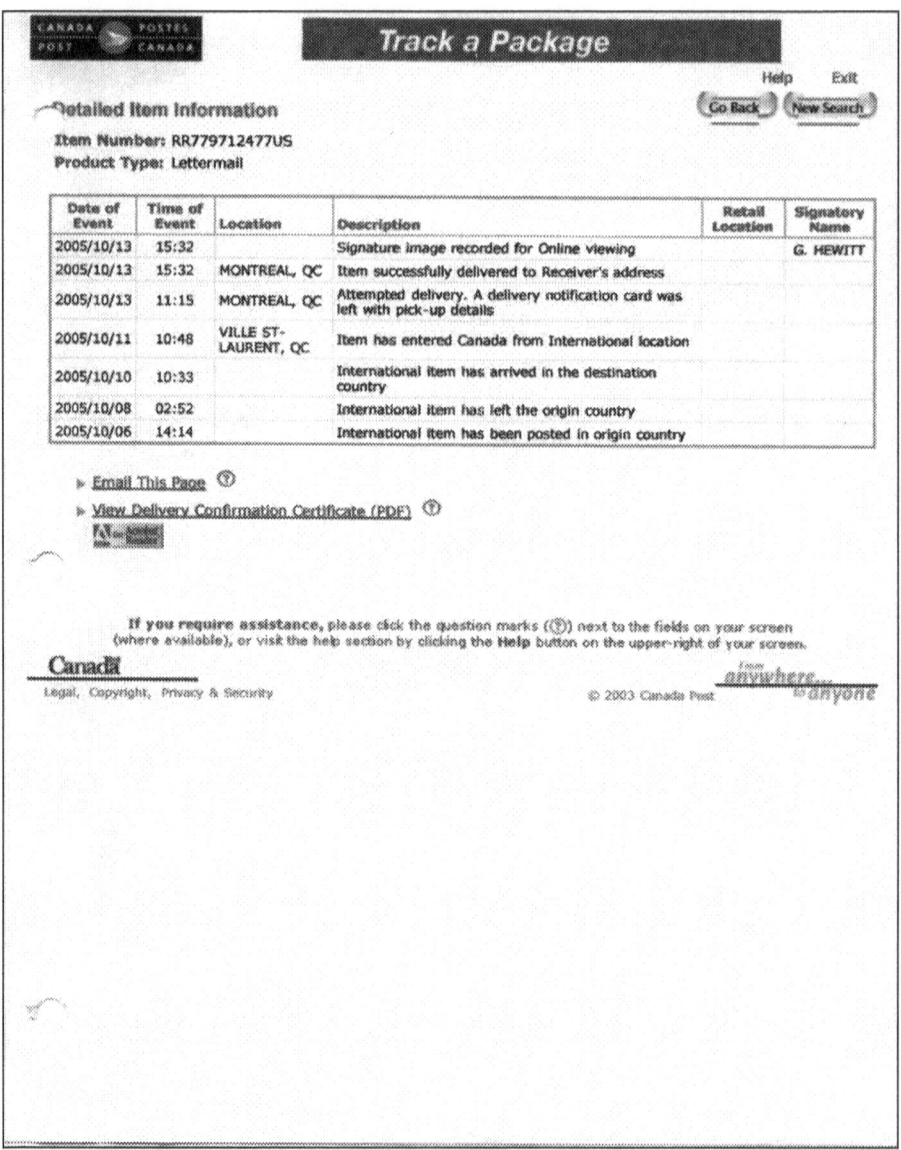

Track a Package

Help   Exit
Go Back   New Search

Detailed Item Information

Item Number: RR779712477US
Product Type: Lettermail

Date of Event	Time of Event	Location	Description	Retail Location	Signatory Name
2005/10/13	15:32		Signature image recorded for Online viewing		G. HEWITT
2005/10/13	15:32	MONTREAL, QC	Item successfully delivered to Receiver's address		
2005/10/13	11:15	MONTREAL, QC	Attempted delivery. A delivery notification card was left with pick-up details		
2005/10/11	10:48	VILLE ST-LAURENT, QC	Item has entered Canada from International location		
2005/10/10	10:33		International item has arrived in the destination country		
2005/10/08	02:52		International item has left the origin country		
2005/10/06	14:14		International item has been posted in origin country		

▸ Email This Page ⑦
▸ View Delivery Confirmation Certificate (PDF) ⑦

If you require assistance, please click the question marks (⑦) next to the fields on your screen (where available), or visit the help section by clicking the **Help** button on the upper-right of your screen.

Canada

Legal, Copyright, Privacy & Security

© 2003 Canada Post

from *anywhere* *to anyone*

#5 includes all the **EMAILS** sent between David and PayPal which you can read earlier in this book.

#6 lists **PayPal Fraud Claims** showing how they purport to prevent fraud. The following item **Item 6A** is text only of the important parts the document called **We Work 24/7 to Protect You.**

PayPal's world-class Fraud Investigation Team stops criminals

PayPal's Fraud Investigation Team is highly experienced in fraud prevention. Several members of the team are former law enforcement officials with extensive experience in fighting online fraud. PayPal's fraud investigation team focuses on:

- **Identifying and preventing fraud before it occurs**
- **Detecting fraud in process**
- **Mitigating loss if fraud does occur**
- **Delivering information to law enforcement around the world to help stop those**

Item 6B entitled **A Wealth of Protection for Our Sellers** attempts to again show how they protect against fraud. However, in David's case, it did not do too well.

State-of-the Art Technology

In addition, PayPal's highly sophisticated fraud models alert us to suspicious account activity and our dedicated anti-fraud teams are trained immediately respond.

More ways PayPal decreases fraud risk:
- Cooperation and shared investigations with the FBI and other law enforcement agencies.

Item 6C, entitled PayPal Fraud Protection, did not protect David.

#7, **Wikipedia information.** http://en.wikipedia.org/wiki/PayPal

#8 Comb v. PayPal is the case where the federal court found PayPal's User Agreement is . . . "substantively unconscionable under California law. . ." This is included starting on p. 51 of this book.

#9 CONSUMER AFFAIRS consists of eight pages of consumer complaints from sellers. They can be found at
http://www.consumeraffairs.com/online/paypal 02.html

#10 PHONE RECORDS consists of copies of phone bills showing calls made regarding this dispute.

#11 COST OF SUIT consists of all records for any money paid out to prosecute the law suit. This will most always include money paid to the process server who served the Summons And Complaint on the defendant as well as the filing fee for filing this claim.

Appendix A
Comb and Toher vs. PayPal, Inc.

IN THE UNITED STATES DISTRICT COURT

FOR THE NORTHERN DISTRICT OF CALIFORNIA

SAN JOSE DIVISION

CRAIG COMB and ROBERTA TOHER, on behalf of themselves and all others similarly situated and on behalf of the general public of the United States, Plaintiffs, v. PAYPAL, INC.,

Defendant. JEFFREY RESNICK, on behalf of himself and all others similarly situated and on behalf of the general public of the United States, Plaintiffs, v. PAYPAL, INC., Defendant.

Case Number   C-02-1227 JF (PVT)

                C-02-2777 JF (PVT)

ORDER   DENYING   MOTIONS   TO   COMPEL INDIVIDUAL ARBITRATION

[Docket No. 23, 5]

Plaintiffs seek injunctive relief and related remedies on behalf of a purported nationwide class for alleged violations of state and federal law by Defendant PayPal, Inc. ("PayPal"). PayPal moves to compel individual arbitration pursuant to the arbitration clause contained in its standard User Agreement and the Federal Arbitration Act ("FAA"), 9 U.S.C. § 1, et seq. The Court has read and considered the moving, responding and supplemental papers as well as the oral arguments presented by counsel on August 12, 2002. For the reasons set forth below, the motions will be denied.[1]

---

[1] On March 29, 2002, the Court determined that the above entitled cases are related pursuant to Civil L.R. 3-12(b).

I. BACKGROUND

A. Customer Complaints

PayPal is an online payment service that allows a business or private individual to send and receive payments via the Internet. A PayPal account holder sends money by informing PayPal of the intended recipient's e-mail address and the amount to be sent and by designating a funding source such as a credit card, bank account or separate PayPal account. PayPal accesses the funds and immediately makes them available to the intended recipient. If an intended recipient does not have a PayPal account, the recipient must open an account to access the payment by following a link that is included in the payment notification e-mail. PayPal generates revenues from transaction fees and the interest it derives from holding funds until they are sent.

As of January 1, 2001, approximately 10,000 account holders had registered with PayPal. PayPal thereafter experienced a sudden and dramatic increase in its popularity, attracting one million customers over the next five months and 10.6 million accounts (of which 8.5 million were held by private individuals) by September 30, 2001. Currently, PayPal provides services to twelve million accounts, and approximately 18,000 new accounts are opened each day. Plaintiffs allege that while PayPal has experienced a seven-fold increase in revenues and a thirteen-fold increase in users, it only has doubled the number of service representatives available to address customer concerns.

Plaintiffs contend that because PayPal's customer base has exceeded its operational capacity, PayPal has been and continues to be unable to maintain and manage accounts in the manner required by applicable state and federal legislation. Plaintiffs allege in particular that when PayPal investigates a customer's complaint of fraud, it freezes the customer's access to his or her account until the investigation is completed, but at the same time keeps the account open for deposits, a practice which allows PayPal to derive economic benefit from the deposits while preventing customers from accessing even undisputed funds while the investigation is pending. Plaintiffs further allege that PayPal does not provide a toll-free customer service telephone number, does not effectively publish the customer service telephone number it does provide, requires customers to report erroneous transactions by e-mail while not providing a specific email address for that purpose, requires customers to provide numerous and burdensome personal documents before it undertakes an investigation, responds to e-mail inquiries with form letters, refuses to provide details or explanations with respect to its investigations, and provides no procedure by which a customer can appeal the results of an investigation. Plaintiffs also allege that when customers *are* able to contact PayPal representatives, the representatives are combative and rude, refuse to answer specific questions, hang up in the middle of phone calls, provide "canned" responses to individualized problems, require customers to fax information while providing inoperative fax numbers, and refuse to allow customers to speak to managers.

Newspaper articles have reported that disgruntled customers who have been unable to contact anyone at PayPal to resolve their disputes have created their own website providing consumers with difficult-to-find customer service numbers and reporting their own frustrations with PayPal's service. According to these accounts, PayPal has a backlog of over 100,000 unanswered customer complaints, a fact that has led the Better Business Bureau to revoke its seal of approval. Plaintiffs allege that PayPal profits from its alleged acts and omissions because customers either abandon their efforts to recover their money or, in cases in which funds actually are returned, because it retains the interest collected on the funds it has held during the investigation process.[2]

1. Craig Comb

Plaintiff Craig Comb ("Comb"), who is not a PayPal customer, alleges the following: On February 15, 2002, without his knowledge, consent or authorization, PayPal removed the sums of $110.00 and $450.00 from his bank account. Comb allegedly had difficulty contacting PayPal with respect to the erroneous transfer and finally reached a PayPal representative on February 18, 2002 to report the alleged error. PayPal acknowledged the error and returned the entire $560.00 to Comb's account on February 25, 2002.

---

[2] PayPal objects to portions of the declarations and supporting exhibits submitted by Plaintiffs Toher and Resnick as vague and ambiguous, irrelevant, improper opinion or conclusion, lacking foundation, and violating the Best Evidence Rule. These objections are overruled.

PayPal's transfers, however, caused Comb's bank account to have insufficient funds, and the bank charged Comb $208.50 for failing to maintain his required balance. Comb contacted PayPal and requested reimbursement for the insufficient fund penalty and any interest his funds accrued while in PayPal's possession. PayPal allegedly refused to pay either amount, disputing Comb's figures but failing to provide Comb its own figures or documentation of its investigation.

2. Roberta Toher

Plaintiff Roberta Toher ("Toher") alleges the following: Toher opened a PayPal account sometime in 2000. PayPal failed to provide her with the name, address, and telephone number of a person she should notify in the event of an unauthorized electronic transfer. On February 24, 2002, Toher discovered that PayPal had transferred funds from her checking account to four individuals without her knowledge, consent or authorization. Toher had difficulty locating any telephone number for contacting PayPal. Once she found a telephone number, which was not toll-free, she was placed on hold for a lengthy period of time, and no one answered her call. Toher then located PayPal's e-mail address and reported the error by e-mail.

On or about February 25, 2002, PayPal responded to Toher by e-mail and instructed her to report the erroneous transaction by sending her complaint to either of two e-mail addresses it provided. Toher sent her complaint to one e-mail address, from which it was returned undeliverable, and then to the other address. She also attempted again to contact PayPal by telephone. After Toher again was placed on hold for a lengthy period of time, a PayPal representative instructed her to change her password and report the error by telephone to a different department. Toher called that department's telephone number and spoke with a service representative who informed her that he had verified that the transaction had not been initiated by Toher and that PayPal would send Toher a letter explaining how to report the transaction in writing. During this time, the recipients who erroneously had received the funds e-mailed Toher and inquired as to the reason for the payment.

On or about February 27, 2002, before her complaint had been investigated or resolved, PayPal informed Toher that it intended to take money from her checking account because her bank had declined a different, unrelated transaction. Toher called PayPal and explained that she had filed a claim with respect to the erroneous withdrawal and instructed PayPal to stop removing funds from the checking account. PayPal explained that there was nothing it could do to stop the latter transaction, and Toher was forced to pay a $27.00 fee to her bank to decline all subsequent electronic transactions related to PayPal. Toher contacted PayPal to request for a second time the letter explaining how to report her original claim. PayPal subsequently informed Toher that it would begin processing her claim once she completed and returned a notarized affidavit by mail.

On March 6, 2002, PayPal sent Toher a series of e-mails explaining that because her bank had declined its attempted transfers, PayPal intended to transfer funds from her credit card account. Toher in turn closed and reopened her credit card account to prevent PayPal from accessing her funds. As of the date the instant suit was filed, PayPal had not acknowledged that Toher had reported an erroneous withdrawal or that an error had occurred, nor had it undertaken any investigation with respect to Toher's complaint.[3]

1. *Jeffrey Resnick*

Plaintiff Jeffrey Resnick ("Resnick") alleges the following: Resnick registered an account with PayPal and linked his e-mail address resnickjeff@hotmail.com (with two "f"s) to that account. He used the account to sell comic books on eBay, an Internet auction service. On January 29, 2002, a third party appropriated Resnick's PayPal user name and password and linked an e-mail account resnickjefff@hotmail.com (with three "f"s) to Resnick's PayPal account. The third party sold two Apple Computers on eBay, and the buyers deposited their payment into the fraudulent account. When the buyers did not receive their product, they filed a complaint with PayPal, which without notice or explanation then restricted Resnick's legitimate account.

In late January or early February 2002, Resnick learned that his account had been restricted and contacted PayPal to inquire as to the reason. Once informed of the circumstances, Resnick explained that he had not sold the computers and stated that because the fraudulent account's email address contained three

---

[3] Although she does not so allege in her complaint, Toher claims in her responding papers that PayPal still holds $136.48 of her money and refuses to return it on the basis that she failed to cooperate with PayPal's investigation. PayPal disputes Toher's allegations and provides the results of its investigation, asserting that Toher's only legitimate claim could be for the return of the $27.00 she elected to pay to her bank to prevent further electronic transfers.

"f"s rather than two, someone must have appropriated his account information. At the time he filed the instant suit, although more than forty-five days had elapsed since he informed PayPal of its error, he had not received any information or documentation with respect to the status of PayPal's investigation, and PayPal had not unrestricted or credited his account.[4]

B. User Agreement

PayPal customers open an account by completing an online application for a personal, premier, or business account. A prospective customer clicks a box at the bottom of the application page that reads, "[you] have read and agree to the User Agreement and [PayPal's] privacy policy." A link to the text of the User Agreement is located at the bottom of the application. The link need not be opened for the application to be processed. The User Agreement is lengthy, consisting of twenty-five printed pages and eleven sections, each containing a number of subparagraphs enumerating the parties' respective obligations and duties.[5]

PayPal admonishes every customer to read the User Agreement carefully, informs him or her that the Agreement forms a binding contract, and advises the customer to retain a copy of the User Agreement.[6]

The User Agreement is a "clickwrap contract," formed when the customer "click[s] 'I Agree,' 'I Accept,' or by submitting payment information through the Service. . . ."

User Agreement, ¶ 2. [7]

---

[4] In its moving papers, PayPal rebuts Resnick's allegations of innocence and provides the results of its investigation.

[5] For purposes of the present motions and unless otherwise noted, all references are to the June 27, 2002 version of the User Agreement submitted with PayPal's moving papers.

[6] The User Agreement begins with the following statement: This User Agreement ("Agreement" or "User Agreement") is a contract between you and PayPal, Inc. and applies to your use of the PayPal™ payment service and any related products and services (collectively the "Service"). This Agreement affects your rights and you should read it carefully. We encourage you to print the Agreement or copy it to your computer's hard drive for your reference.

[7] ¶ 2 provides that:[Y]ou agree to the terms and conditions of this Agreement, the PayPal Privacy Policy, and any documents incorporated by reference. You further agree that this User Agreement forms a legally binding contract between you and PayPal, and that this Agreement constitutes "a writing signed by You" under any applicable law or regulation.

The User Agreement contains the following arbitration clause:

Arbitration. Any controversy or claim arising out of or relating to this Agreement or the provision of Services shall be settled by binding arbitration in accordance with the commercial arbitration rules of the American Arbitration Association. Any such controversy or claim shall be arbitrated on an individual basis, and shall not be consolidated in any arbitration with any claim or controversy of any other party. The arbitration shall be conducted in Santa Clara County, California, and judgment on the arbitration award may be entered in any court having jurisdiction thereof. Either you or PayPal may seek any interim or preliminary relief from a court of competent jurisdiction in Santa Clara County, California necessary to protect the rights or property of you or PayPal, Inc. (or its agents, suppliers, and subcontractors) pending the completion of arbitration.

User Agreement, Section II (19).

II. DISCUSSION

The FAA was enacted to overcome longstanding judicial reluctance to enforce agreements to arbitrate. Bradley v. Harris Research, Inc., 275 F.3d 884, 888 (9th Cir. 2001). It applies to all written contracts involving interstate or foreign commerce and provides in relevant part that arbitration agreements contained within such contracts "shall be valid, irrevocable, and enforceable, save upon such grounds as exist at law or in equity for the revocation of any contract." 9 U.S.C. § 2. "The FAA creates a body of federal substantive law of arbitrability, enforceable in both state and federal courts and pre-empting any state laws or policies to the contrary." Ticknor v. Choice Hotels Int'l, Inc., 265 F.3d 931, 936 (9th Cir. 2001) (citations and internal quotation omitted). As a result, state laws hostile to arbitration agreements have been held invalid on the ground that such laws frustrate congressional intent to place arbitration agreements on the same footing as other contracts. Bradley, 275 F.3d at 889.

State law is not entirely displaced from FAA analysis, however. It is undisputed that "generally applicable contract defenses, such as fraud, duress, or unconscionability, may be applied to invalidate arbitration agreements without contravening § 2."

Doctor's Assocs., Inc. v. Casarotto, 517 U.S. 681, 686 (1996).
Here, the User Agreement is "governed by and interpreted under
the laws of the state of California . . . [as] applied to agreements
entered into and to be performed entirely within California by
California residents." User Agreement, Section II (18). Because
there is no dispute that the contract at issue in this case involves
interstate commerce, this Court's role thus is limited to
determining whether under California law (1) a valid agreement
to arbitrate exists and, if so, (2) whether the agreement
encompasses the dispute at issue. See Chiron Corp. v. Ortho
Diagnostic Sys., Inc., 207 F.3d 1126, 1130 (9th Cir. 2000). If
both of these requirements are satisfied, the FAA requires this
Court to enforce the subject arbitration clause in accordance
with the terms of the User Agreement. Id.

A.   **Agreement to Arbitrate**

Even though California has a strong policy favoring arbitration,
"[i]t is beyond cavil that arbitration is a matter of contract and a
party cannot be required to submit to arbitration any dispute
which he has not agreed so to submit." Ajida Tech., Inc., v. Roos
Instruments, Inc., 87 Cal.App.4th 534, 541 (2001) (citations
and internal quotation omitted). The Court must interpret the
parties' written agreement so as to give effect to the parties'
mutual intention. Ben-Zvi v. Edmar Co., 40 Cal.App.4th 468,
473 (1995); Floystrup v. City of Berkeley Rent Stabilization Bd.,
219 Cal.App.3d 1309, 1317 (1990). If possible, the Court will
determine the parties' intention solely from the language of the
agreement itself. Ben-Zvi, 40 Cal.App.4th at 473. Extrinsic
evidence is admissible, however, if the offered evidence is
relevant to prove the meaning of ambiguous language and such
interpretation is reasonable in light of all the facts,
circumstances, and conditions surrounding the execution of the
agreement. Oakland-Alameda County Coliseum v. Oakland
Raiders, Ltd., 197 Cal.App.3d 1049, 1057-58 (1988). "Because
the existence of the agreement is a statutory prerequisite to
granting the petition, the petitioner bears the burden of proving
its existence by a preponderance of the evidence." Rosenthal v.
Great W. Fin. Securities Corp.,14 Cal.4th 394, 413 (1996).

It is undisputed that Comb's claims are not subject to
arbitration. With respect to Toher and Resnick, PayPal failed to
submit with its original moving papers copies of the agreements
into which Toher and Resnick allegedly entered, arguing that
circumstantial evidence sufficiently demonstrates assent by these
Plaintiffs to the User Agreement PayPal currently offers its new

customers. At oral argument, PayPal reiterated its claim that Resnick entered into an agreement containing the exact arbitration clause found in Section II (19) of the current User Agreement, but it conceded that the version of the User Agreement entered into by Toher did not contain the subject arbitration clause. PayPal nonetheless argued that Toher is bound to the *current* User Agreement, including the arbitration clause, because the version of the User Agreement Toher did accept binds her to any subsequent revisions to the User Agreement. After the hearing, PayPal submitted supplemental declarations and exhibits ("the Supplemental Material") from PayPal's Senior Manager for Online Communications and Marketing Damon Billian.[8] The Supplemental Material provides an electronic record of the dates Toher and Resnick opened their respective accounts, a copy of the version of the User Agreement PayPal claims was in effect at the time the respective accounts were opened, and copies of five subsequent versions of the User Agreement.

Although an electronic record constitutes sufficient evidence that the parties have entered into a binding agreement, the applicable statutes require production of *a record* that the parties have entered into an agreement and evidence of the terms and conditions contained in such agreement. Plaintiffs argue that the Supplemental Material contains no evidence of any electronic or actual record of Plaintiffs' assent to the purported agreements. The Court agrees that PayPal has made a weak showing, but for purposes of the instant motion, it will assume without deciding that the circumstantial evidence is sufficient to demonstrate that Toher and Resnick entered into agreements with PayPal.[9]

---

[8] Plaintiffs object strenuously to the Court's consideration of the Supplemental Material. They argue that PayPal filed these documents in violation of this Court's Local Rules, and that the documents demonstrate that PayPal's original claim that Toher agreed to arbitration was false. The Court agrees that the filing did not comply with the Local Rules, and one reasonably may infer from the circumstances that PayPal's counsel at the very least were negligent in their original representations to the Court. The Court does not take such irregularities lightly and will not hesitate to impose sanctions should this situation arise again. Nonetheless, because it concludes that the interests of justice are best served by reaching Plaintiffs' unconscionability arguments, the Court has given counsel the benefit of the doubt and has considered the Supplemental Material.

[9] PayPal argues that because the User Agreement entered into by Toher provides that "this Agreement is subject to change at any time without notice," she assented to the arbitration clause that PayPal inserted into a subsequent version of the User Agreement. In light of the disposition of the motion, the Court need not decide whether such a provision ever could result in a binding agreement to arbitrate. As discussed below,

B.   Unconscionability

Plaintiffs argue that even if they did enter into a version of the User Agreement, the User Agreement and in particular its arbitration clause are unconscionable. Unconscionability is a defense applicable to contracts generally and thus may be raised in defense to an arbitration provision. Blake v. Ecker, 93 Cal.App.4th 728, 741 (2001). Unconscionability has both procedural and substantive components. Id. at 742. The procedural component is satisfied by the existence of unequal bargaining positions and hidden terms common in the context of adhesion contracts. Id. The substantive component is satisfied by overly harsh or one-sided results that "shock the conscience." Id. The two elements operate on a sliding scale such that the more significant one is, the less significant the other need be. Id. at 743. A claim of unconscionability cannot be determined merely by examining the face of the contract; there must be an inquiry into the circumstances under which the contract was executed, its purpose, and effect. Id.

1. Procedural Unconscionability

A contract or clause is procedurally unconscionable if it is a contract of adhesion. Flores v. Transamerica HomeFirst, Inc., 93 Cal.App.4th 846, 853 (2001). A contract of adhesion, in turn, is a "standardized contract, which, imposed and drafted by the party of superior bargaining strength, relegates to the subscribing party only the opportunity to adhere to the contract or reject it." Armendariz v. Foundation Health Psychcare Serv., 24 Cal.4th 83, 113 (2000) (citations and internal quotation omitted). Although PayPal does not dispute that the agreement and arbitration clause at issue here meet this definition, it asserts that the instant contract is not procedurally unconscionable because it does not concern essential items such as food or clothing and because Plaintiffs had meaningful alternative sources for the subject services. Relying upon Dean Witter Reynolds, Inc. v. Superior Court, 211 Cal.App.3d 758, 769 (1989), PayPal argues that the availability of alternative sources is enough to defeat a showing of procedural unconscionability. In Dean Witter, however, the California Court of Appeal noted that the party asserting unconscionability was "a sophisticated investor" and that "[t]he record establishe[d] without conflict that other

---

however, PayPal's unilateral and apparently unfettered right to revise the User Agreement does bear on the question of whether the User Agreement is substantively unconscionable.

financial institutions offered competing IRA's which lacked the challenged provision." Id. at 771. In this case, the amount of the average transaction is $55.00, the vast majority of PayPal customers are private individuals who are not "sophisticated," and there is at least a factual dispute as to whether PayPal's competitors offer their services without requiring customers to enter into arbitration agreements.[10] The Dean Witter court explicitly limited its holding, indicating that a claim of procedural unconscionability cannot be defeated merely by "*any* showing of competition in the marketplace as to the desired goods and services. . . ." Id. at 772 (emphasis in original). PayPal cites no authority extending Dean Witter to circumstances analogous to those presented here. Cf. Armendariz, 24 Cal.4th at 113 (rejecting argument that contract between employer and employee was not adhesive because employer demonstrated existence of alternative sources of employment that were not conditioned on the acceptance of an arbitration clause). See also, Szetela v. Discover Bank, 97 Cal.App.4th 1094, 1100 (2002) (finding availability of substitute goods not "the relevant test for unconscionability" in dispute between unsophisticated consumer and large financial institution). The Court concludes that the User Agreement at issue here satisfies the criteria for procedural unconscionability under California law.

2. Substantive Unconscionability

Even if instant agreement is procedurally unconscionable, it may nonetheless be enforceable if the substantive terms are reasonable. See Craig v. Brown & Root, Inc., 84 Cal.App.4th 416, 422-23 (2000) (finding contract of adhesion to arbitrate disputes enforceable). The Court's principal substantive concerns in the present case are a lack of mutuality in the User Agreement and the practical effects of the arbitration clause with respect to consolidation of claims, the costs of arbitration, and venue.

a. Mutuality

Substantive unconscionability has been found in many cases based upon arbitration provisions requiring arbitration of the weaker party's claims but permitting a choice of forums for the stronger party. See, e.g., Ticknor, 265 F.3d at 940-41; Mercuro

---

[10] The record also demonstrates that individuals who are not account holders must register with the service as a precondition to accessing funds that an account holder sends to them. Although none of the named Plaintiffs opened an account by such means, the Court notes that such individuals would not have any meaningful alternatives available to them.

v. Superior Court, 96 Cal.App.4th 167, 176 (2002). Considered in isolation, the arbitration clause at issue here appears to permit a mutuality of remedies, providing that "[e]ither you or PayPal may seek any interim or preliminary relief from a court of competent jurisdiction in Santa Clara County, California necessary to protect the rights or property of you or PayPal, Inc. (or its agents, suppliers, and subcontractors) pending the completion of arbitration." User Agreement, Section II (19). Section V(3) of the User Agreement, however, provides that in the event of a dispute, PayPal "at its sole discretion" may restrict accounts, withhold funds, undertake its own investigation of a customer's financial records, close accounts, and procure ownership of all funds in dispute unless and until the customer is "later determined to be entitled to the funds in dispute." PayPal alone makes the final decision with respect to a dispute.[11] Finally, as noted earlier, the User Agreement "is subject to change by PayPal without prior notice (unless prior notice is required by law), by posting of the revised Agreement on the PayPal website."[12] A contract may provide a "margin of safety" that

---

[11] Section V(3) provides: PayPal, at its sole discretion, reserves the right to close an account at any time for any reason, including but not limited to a violation of this Agreement, upon notice to the User and payment to the User of any unrestricted funds held in custody. PayPal, at its sole discretion, also reserves the right to periodically retrieve and review a business and / or consumer credit report for any account, and reserves the right to close an account based on information obtained during this credit review process. PayPal, at its sole discretion, also reserves the right to restrict withdrawals from an account for any one of the events listed below. If the dispute covers only a specific transaction, we will only restrict funds related to that particular transaction. If your account is restricted, you will be notified by e-mail and requested to provide information relevant to your account. PayPal will investigate the matter promptly. If the investigation is in your favor, we will unrestrict your account. If the investigation is not in your favor, PayPal may return funds to the sender and unrestrict the remainder of your account, continue the restriction for up to 180 days as to funds necessary to protect PayPal against the risk of reversals, or may close your account by giving you notice and mailing a check for any funds in your account (minus funds that are in dispute) to the address that you have provided. If you are later determined to be entitled to the funds in dispute, PayPal will make an additional payment of those funds to you. Any of the following events may lead to a restriction of your account . . . .[omitting list of nineteen provisions that include "Receipt of potentially fraudulent funds," "Refusal to cooperate in an investigation," "Opening multiple Personal accounts," and "Logging in from a country not included on PayPal's permitted countries list."]. . . .[¶] PayPal will use reasonable efforts to investigate accounts that are subject to a restriction and to reach a final decision promptly.

[12] ¶ 2 provides:

This Agreement is subject to change by PayPal without prior notice (unless prior notice is required by law), by posting of the revised Agreement on the PayPal website. Descriptions of material amendments to this Agreement will be posted in advance on the PayPal website in the "Policy Updates" section that is displayed to you when you log in to your account. You can also set your Preferences to receive e-mail notification of all policy updates. You may review the current Agreement prior to initiating a transaction at any time at our User Agreement page.

provides the party with superior bargaining strength protection for which it has a legitimate commercial need. "However, unless the 'business realities' that create the special need for such an advantage are explained in the contract itself, . . . it must be factually established." Stirlen v. Supercuts, Inc., 51 Cal.App.4th 1519, 1536 (1997). When a contract is alleged to be unconscionable, "the parties shall be afforded a reasonable opportunity to present evidence as to its commercial setting, purpose, and effect to aid the court in making the determination." Cal. Civ. Code § 1670.5. The statutory scheme reflects "legislative recognition that a claim of unconscionability often cannot be determined merely by examining the face of the contract, but will require inquiry into its setting, purpose, and effect." <u>Stirlen</u>, 51 Cal.App.4th at 1536 (citations and internal quotations omitted).

PayPal argues that the User Agreement does not lack mutuality because nothing in the agreement precludes a customer from using the court system to seek any relief related to a restricted account pending the outcome of an arbitration proceeding. However, Plaintiffs present evidence that PayPal has frozen customer accounts and retained funds that it alone determined were subject to dispute without notice to the named Plaintiffs. The User Agreement expressly authorizes PayPal to engage in such conduct unilaterally. While in theory a customer may seek provisional relief in the courts, including presumably an order to unfreeze an account, the cost of doing so would be prohibitive in relation to the amounts typically in dispute. For all practical purposes, a customer may resolve disputes only after PayPal has had control of the disputed funds for an indefinite period of time. Although PayPal alone may amend the User Agreement without notice or negotiation, a customer is bound to any and all such amendments for the duration of the customer's relationship with PayPal. PayPal has not shown that "business realities" justify such one-sidedness. <u>See, e.g,</u> <u>Flores</u>, 93 Cal.App.4th at 854 (finding lack of mutuality when debtor must arbitrate any controversy arising out of a loan whereas the lender may proceed by judicial or nonjudicial foreclosure, by self-help remedies such as setoff, and by injunctive relief to obtain appointment of a receiver); <u>Stirlin</u>, 51 Cal.App.4th at 1540 (finding that a mandatory arbitration requirement realistically applies "primarily if not exclusively" to claims filed by the employer in light of employer's failure to identify any provision of the contract or statute likely to give rise to a claim to which it would be compelled to submit to arbitration).

b. **Prohibition against Consolidation of Claims**

The subject arbitration clause expressly prohibits PayPal customers from consolidating their claims. Relying upon <u>Vernon v. Drexel Burnham & Co.</u>, 52 Cal.App.3d 706, 716 (1975), PayPal argues that such a prohibition cannot render an agreement to arbitrate substantively unconscionable. The arbitration clause in <u>Vernon</u>, however, did not preclude consolidation of claims *per se*, and whatever relevance <u>Vernon</u> may have in this case is overshadowed by the much more recent decision of the California Court of Appeal in <u>Szetela v Discover Bank</u>, 97 Cal.App.4th at 1094. As is this case here, the arbitration agreement at issue in Szetela categorically prohibited individual customers from joining or consolidating claims in arbitration. The court determined that a large credit card company could not enforce the prohibition with respect to consumer claims against it because in practice most claims likely would involve consumers seeking the return of small amounts of money, and any remedy obtained by the few consumers who would not be dissuaded from pursuing their rights would pertain only to those consumers without collateral estoppel effect. <u>Id</u>. at 1101. The court concluded that such circumstances raise "[t]he potential for millions of customers to be overcharged small amounts without an effective method of redress. . . ." <u>Id</u>.

PayPal argues that because federal cases applying the FAA have enforced arbitration clauses containing such prohibitions on collective actions,[13] <u>Szetela</u> is irrelevant to the present proceedings. In the Ninth Circuit, however, while the FAA preempts any legislation "specifically aimed at arbitration agreements," "[i]n all situations where arbitration provisions are placed on the same footing as other contracts, state law applies." <u>Ticknor</u>, 265 F.3d at 941 (citation and internal quotation omitted). Thus, while California's consumer protection statutes cannot prevent enforcement under the FAA of a prohibition on collective actions as such, a federal court properly may consider whether such a prohibition in combination with other provisions and circumstances renders an agreement substantively unconscionable as a matter of state law.

---

[13] <u>See, e.g., Champ v. Siegel Trading Co.</u>, 55 F.3d 269, 274-75 (7th Cir. 1995); <u>Gilmer v. Interstate/Johnson Lane Corp.</u>, 500 U.S. 20, 32 (1991).

Costs of Arbitration

Plaintiffs claim that the cost of an individual arbitration under the User Agreement is likely to exceed $5,000 and submit declarations stating that such arbitration would be cost-prohibitive for them.14 PayPal disputes Plaintiffs' calculation of costs, contending that because any arbitration in practice would proceed under the consumer rules of the American Arbitration Association ("AAA"), a customer's only expense would be a filing fee of approximately $125.00.

The arbitration clause itself expressly undercuts PayPal's assertion. It states in pertinent part that "[a]ny controversy or claim arising out of or relating to this Agreement or the provision of Services shall be settled by binding arbitration in accordance with the *commercial* arbitration rules of the American Arbitration Association." (emphasis added).[15] Further, because the clause is silent as to who bears the cost of arbitration, under California law each party is required to pay a *pro rata* share of the "expenses and fees of the neutral arbitrator, together with other expenses of the arbitration incurred or approved by the neutral arbitrator, not including counsel fees or witness fees or other expenses incurred by a party for his own benefit." Cal. Code Civ. P. § 1284.2.

Unlike the plaintiff in <u>Green Tree Fin. Corp.-Ala. v. Randolph</u>, 531 U.S. 79 (2000) who claimed that the unknown and unidentified risk of excessive fees should be sufficient to defeat a valid arbitration clause, the named Plaintiffs here, none of whose individual claims exceeds $310.00, have shown that the costs each of them is likely to incur in commercial arbitration likely would exceed those involved in bringing a collective action. By allowing for prohibitive arbitration fees and precluding joinder of claims (which would make each individual customer's participation in arbitration more economical), PayPal appears to be attempting to insulate itself contractually from any meaningful challenge to its alleged practices. Under these

---

[14] PayPal objects to the declaration of Ann Saponora as exceeding the page limitations applicable to Plaintiffs' opposing papers and object to various portions of the declaration as vague and ambiguous, irrelevant, lacking foundation, hearsay, improper opinion, conclusion, speculation, violating the Best Evidence Rule, and improper use of case law and argument in a declaration. The objections are overruled. <u>See also, supra,</u> n.2.

[15] The AAA rules, offered in evidence by PayPal at oral argument, plainly contain distinct procedures for "commercial" and "consumer" arbitrations.

circumstances, the Court concludes that this aspect of the arbitration clause is so harsh as to be substantively unconscionable. See, e.g., Armendariz, 24 Cal.4th at 113.

d. Venue

The User Agreement requires that any arbitration take place in Santa Clara County, California. PayPal argues that this venue provision is not unconscionable because forum selection clauses in general are *prima facie* valid, courts have found similar forum selection clauses in arbitration clauses reasonable, and the named Plaintiffs themselves elected to litigate in this Court, thereby undercutting any claim that the contractual forum is burdensome or inconvenient for them. Although it is true that forum selection clauses generally are presumed *prima facie* valid, a forum selection clause may be unconscionable if the "place or manner" in which arbitration is to occur is unreasonable taking into account "the respective circumstances of the parties." Bolter v. Superior Court, 87 Cal.App.4th 900, 909 (2001). The record in this case shows that PayPal serves millions of customers across the United States and that the amount of the average transaction through PayPal is $55.00. Although PayPal cites to unpublished or out-of-state authority holding that such facts do not warrant a finding of unconscionability, PayPal cites no California authority holding that it is reasonable for individual consumers from throughout the country to travel to one locale to arbitrate claims involving such minimal sums. Limiting venue to PayPal's backyard appears to be yet one more means by which the arbitration clause serves to shield PayPal from liability instead of providing a neutral forum in which to arbitrate disputes.[16] See, e.g., Bolter, 87 Cal.App.4th at 909 (finding that enforcement of forum selection clause providing that claims are arbitrated exclusively in Utah would be cost prohibitive in light of fact that the potential claimants located around the country would be required to retain counsel familiar with Utah law).[17]

---

[16] As it does with respect to the costs of arbitration, PayPal contends that the AAA consumer rules mitigate any unfairness by permitting telephonic participation in arbitration hearings. As already discussed, however, the User Agreement on its face provides that the AAA commercial rules apply.

[17] Plaintiffs also contend that the subject arbitration clause is unconscionable because it requires them to waive statutory rights. The Court does not find this contention persuasive, and in any event it need not reach it.

III. DISPOSITION

Having considered the terms of the User Agreement generally and the arbitration clause in particular, as well as the totality of the circumstances, the Court concludes that the User Agreement and arbitration clause are substantively unconscionable under California law and that arbitration cannot be compelled herein. Good cause therefore appearing, IT IS HEREBY ORDERED that the motions to compel individual arbitration are DENIED.

DATED: August 30, 2002

/s/ (electronic signature authorized)

JEREMY FOGEL

United States District Judge

Copies of Order mailed on _____ to:

Patricia I. Avery

David J. Brown

Michael Shawn Connell

Daniel C. Girard

David S. Harris

Stephanie Johnson

Molly Moriarty Lane

Gary A. Peterson

The Trial

SUPERIOR COURT OF THE STATE OF CALIFORNIA
FOR THE COUNTY OF LOS ANGELES

DIVISION 1

HONORABLE EDWARD H. DRAYER, COMMISSIONER

HEIDI BEZAIRE AND DAVID BEZAIRE   Case No. 05S01609
Plaintiffs

vs. PAYPAL, INC.

Defendant

SMALL CLAIMS HEARING

March 6, 2006

APPEARANCES:

FOR THE PLAINTIFF: HEIDI BEZAIRE, pro per DAVID BEZAIRE, pro per

FOR THE DEFENDANT: MICHELLE SQUIRES

TRANSCRIPTION BY: *Lutz & Company, Inc.*
100 West Lemon Avenue Suite 103
Monrovia, California 91016 (626) 303-1113
Info@lutz-co.com

Proceedings recorded by an unmonitored electronic sound recording, transcript produced by Federally Approved Transcription Service.

BELLFLOWER, CALIFORNIA

MONDAY, MARCH 6, 2006, PROCEEDINGS BEGIN

DIVISION 1, HONORABLE EDWARD H. DRAYER,

COMMISSIONER

(Court is Called to Order)

THE COURT: Okay. Call the matter of Heidi Bezaire, also named Plaintiff David Bezaire versus PayPal, Incorporated.

(Pause)

THE COURT: All right. We have Mr. and Mrs. Bezaire, is that correct?

PLAINTIFF H. BEZAIRE: Yes. PLAINTIFF D. BEZAIRE: Yes.

THE COURT: And then you're here on behalf of the defendant, PayPal, Incorporated?

MS. SQUIRES: That's correct.

THE COURT: Could you state your name for the record please.

MS. SQUIRES: Michelle Squires.

THE COURT: You're authorized to testify for the corporation?

MS. SQUIRES: Yes, I am. *(Author's note: Remember this.)*

THE COURT: Okay. Well the first thing I want to take up is the issue of venue. And as I recall the last time the case was here PayPal had sent a letter in and you both agreed to continue the case to today and I believe you told me you were going to submit some, some cases regarding the letter that was sent to them. So the first thing is, is venue only. So now this is PayPal's motion for a change of venue. What would you like to say in that regard, Ma'am?

MS. SQUIRES: In order to create a PayPal account a person has to agree to our user agreement and it very clearly states that it's a contract and that if you do not choose to abide by the terms and conditions then you should not

69

use our services. And David Bezaire created his account and accepted our user agreement. And --

THE COURT: Where's the user agreement?

MS. SQUIRES: I have –

THE COURT: Pardon?

MS. SQUIRES: --documents right here for you.

THE COURT: Okay. All right.

MS. SQUIRES: David Bezaire created this account not Heidi so I object to her arguing this case.

THE COURT: Pardon me?

MS. SQUIRES: I think that she doesn't have a claim in this case. The account is registered just in David Bezaire's name not in her name.

THE COURT: Well, I mean, if, if the plaintiff isn't a proper party then I dismiss them from the case.

MS. SQUIRES: Okay.

THE COURT: But I'm going to let everybody be heard. In fact I'd --I made some extra efforts so you could be heard today. I believe there's another case for you too. So if people made the trek down here to be witnesses, everybody gets a chance to be heard.

MS. SQUIRES: All righty.

THE COURT: Is that fair enough?

MS. SQUIRES: That's fair.

THE COURT: Okay. The rules are going to apply for everybody. I'll mark these defense exhibits. What else would you like --tell me?

(Defendant's Exhibit, Marked)

MS. SQUIRES: So when he accepted this user agreement, that means that he accepted Section 15, which is our legal dispute clause and in the dispute clause you're afforded two forums to bring a legal dispute.

THE COURT: Okay. Now I'm, I'm holding this, can you point to what page of the documents you've submitted this would be on.

MS. SQUIRES: There's a pink tab and it should be on Page 6 or 7.

THE COURT: A pink tab. This --it says, two of thirteen.

MS. SQUIRES: That's saying that it's a contract and that and you agree to abide by the terms and conditions --

THE COURT: Okay. How would he get a copy of this?

MS. SQUIRES: He has to review that before he can create his account.

THE COURT: Okay.

MS. SQUIRES: It's all done on-line.

THE COURT: Okay. Go ahead.

MS. SQUIRES: And then if you turn to the --second pink tab, that's Section 15, that shows that you are afforded two forums for legal dispute. The first one would be arbitration where no one has to travel and the second one is litigation in Santa Clara County, California.

So I explained this to Mr. Bezaire both on the phone and then I followed. up in writing which is provided Form 15.4 and he failed to withdraw this claim so I believe that he should have this case --we should have this case dismissed and that I should be reimbursed for having to travel here from San Jose, California to enforce the user agreement.

THE COURT: Anything further.

MS. SQUIRES: I believe that they're going to bring up a case that was litigated in 2002, it's the <u>Comb</u> case. Originally our user agreement afforded face to face arbitration in Palo Alto, California. And the 2002 case was in the context of a class action and the judge, Jeremy Fogel, ruled that our user agreement should not be enforced. But that was because it was a class action and he did not feel it was fair to force people to arbitrate in Palo Alto, California when the average cost of our on-line payment was fifty dollars ($50).

But that's clearly not the case here. The <u>Comb</u> case did not address venue and Mr. Bezaire's claim is for one thousand four hundred thirty-four dollars ($1,434) which is way more than the fifty dollars ($50). And in fact I believe that plaintiff has increased his claim another three thousand dollars ($3,000) for punitive damages. This was --I was noticed of this through a handwritten note after the claim was filed.

And I may be --incorrect but I don't think that punitive damages are allowed in small claims court but they're certainly not allowed in our user agreement. In fact our user --agreement clearly states that you are only allowed to sue us for actual damages not consequential damages. This <u>Comb</u> case is currently on appeal in the 9th Circuit and we believe it's going to be reversed. *(Author's note: Remember that statement.)*

But in the mean time as a result of Judge Fogel's decision we expanded our user agreement and the legal dispute clause so that people could arbitrate where no one had to travel or they could litigate in Santa Clara County. And Mr. Bezaire agreed to this new user agreement on March 8, 2003, so he should be held to the terms of 15, Section 15.

THE COURT: All right. Now I'm looking at their claim and it's for fourteen hundred thirty-four dollars ($1,434), you said they've amended it?

MS. SQUIRES: Well they haven't amended their complaint, they told me that they're increasing it by three thousand dollars ($3,000) for punitive damages but it's --I've not received an official amended complaint. I did warn him that if he wanted to increase it he'd probably need to file amended complaint.

THE COURT: All right. Anything else? Just on the venue issue at this point.

MS. SQUIRES: No.

THE COURT: All right. Okay. Then who'd like to speak first on the --this is on the venue only at this point?

PLAINTIFF D. BEZAIRE: I would, Your Honor.

THE COURT: Okay.

PLAINTIFF D. BEZAIRE: We'd like to submit U.S. District Court case <u>Comb v. PayPal,</u> we believe that it clearly states that the venue provision in the user agreement is unconscionable and unenforceable.

THE COURT: Okay. Is that the case there?

PLAINTIFF D. BEZAIRE: This is.

THE COURT: Okay. Can you hand that to the bailiff? PLAINTIFF D. BEZAIRE: Okay. And we've highlighted a section --there's a section -- specifically titled venue that addresses this and that highlighted portion in under that section.

THE COURT: And what?

PLAINTIFF D. BEZAIRE: There's a highlighted portion on page --

THE COURT: Okay. It's, it's all in here though, right?

PLAINTIFF D. BEZAIRE: Yes.

THE COURT: Okay.

PLAINTIFF H. BEZAIRE: On Page 17 of the highlighted section.

(Pause)

THE COURT: All right. Okay. Anything further?

PLAINTIFF D. BEZAIRE: No, Your Honor.

THE COURT: Okay. All right. Did you wish to say anything, Ma'am?

MS. SQUIRES: No. That's pretty much --so we feel that this is properly filed in the proper venue.

THE COURT: Okay. All right. Then did you have a chance to review --I asked all the parties to exchange exhibits, did you happen to look at that?

MS. SQUIRES: Yes, I did.

THE COURT: All right. Now do you feel that that addresses venue?

MS. SQUIRES: Again, that case addressed whether or not there should be a --prohibition of class action being forced to arbitrate face to face in California in Palo Alto. The Court ruled that it was not and that's fine. They expanded our -- provisions but it did not address whether venue was improper. The judge essentially felt that it was proper to allow users to file as a class and – *(Author's note: Please tell me how she came to this conclusion.)*

THE COURT: Well but you have to, you know, somehow you have to get it declared as a class action which is not automatically done.

MS. SQUIRES: Okay. But this is not --

THE COURT: You just can't walk down to the courthouse and say I'm filing a class action, other --there needs to be certain findings. Weren't there certain findings in, in that case as a class action? You know, I haven't read the case. I'm going, I'm going to read the whole thing before I make any ruling.

MS. SQUIRES: Okay.

THE COURT: But if you're familiar with the case, wasn't there some procedure that went through to make it a class action?

MS. SQUIRES: I, I can't address that, I'm sorry. *(Author's note: Why can she not address that? She seems to know all about the case. Or is this simply another smoke and mirror trick to make this case disappear? We will look at that further down.)*

THE COURT: Okay.

MS. SQUIRES: All I know is that venue is different than the class action part of it.

THE COURT: Okay. All right. Okay. Anything else?

MS. SQUIRES: No.

THE COURT: Okay. All right. Then, sir, let me just ask, are -- do you intend to amend your lawsuit? I only see a claim of fourteen hundred and thirty-four dollars ($1,434).

PLAINTIFF D. BEZAIRE: No, Your Honor. We don't intend to amend the lawsuit. We, we'll stick to the fourteen hundred and thirty-four dollars ($1,434) .

THE COURT: All right. Okay. Let me pass this and call the next case. I've, I've got to read all this before I can make any ruling on venue. So if you'll all just have a seat there. Not --just the Bezaire's.

(Whereupon the Court Hears Another Matter)

THE COURT: All right. Let me recall Mr. and Mrs. Bezaire's matter versus PayPal.

All right. I have reviewed all the material submitted by both sides. One of the matters that --of concern to me is that you're relying on the Comb case and it's been submitted that the Comb case is currently on appeal. When a case is on appeal quite often it doesn't --not quite often, but it doesn't --it's not settled law at that point in time. There's a possibility, I'm not saying it's going to get reversed but there's a possibility that the case could be reversed. Do any of you know when that case might be heard by the Ninth Circuit, sir? *(Author's note: Of course nobody knows because as you will see later, the case IS NOT on appeal.)*

PLAINTIFF D. BEZAIRE: We don't know.

PLAINTIFF H. BEZAIRE: We weren't aware it was under appeal.

THE COURT: Pardon?

PLAINTIFF H. BEZAIRE: We weren't aware that it was under appeal.

THE COURT: Well that's what's written here and is —

MS. SQUIRE: It's true.

THE COURT: --that your understanding?

MS. SQUIRE: That is true. *(**Author's note: How can she make such preposterous statements when the case was not up on appeal as you will soon learn?**)*

THE COURT: And I think you mentioned in your presentation that you thought it was going to get reversed.

PLAINTIFF D. BEZAIRE: (Inaudible).

THE COURT: Okay. Well here's what I'd be willing to do. We're trying to accommodate you so you don't have to come back. And I know you folks have come back. I'd take the issue of venue under submission but I'd hear the facts of the case today. Now, if later I rule that the venue's not proper then can't render a judgment. Would that be agreeable to everybody.

PLAINTIFF H. BEZAIRE: Yes, Your Honor.

MS. SQUIRES: Fine by me. Sure, that's fair.

THE COURT: Okay. All right. But understand I still haven't made a ruling on, on the venue, okay?

MS. SQUIRES: Sure.

THE COURT: All right. So, so what would you like to tell me? And then let's take one other thing up. Ma'am, were you a party to it at all other than just being the spouse of Mr. Bezaire?

PLAINTIFF H. BEZAIRE: Uh-huh. Yes, sir. We've been --we weren't quite sure how to file,

THE COURT: Uh-huh.

PLAINTIFF H. BEZAIRE: --both names or just one.

THE COURT: Uh-huh.

PLAINTIFF H. BEZAIRE: The account is under Dave's name. The reason why I'm involved is I was very involved in trying to resolve this issue as it played out --

THE COURT: Okay. Well you can be a witness to that, right?

PLAINTIFF H. BEZAIRE: Sure. Well I guess --

THE COURT: But it's really his account, is that correct?

PLAINTIFF D. BEZAIRE: It was my account, however --

THE COURT: Okay. Is it a joint account or a separate account?

PLAINTIFF D. BEZAIRE: It's a separate account, however, the financial loss was really suffered by Heidi because what was sold on Ebay was hers.

THE COURT: Okay. Well I'll, I'll listen to the facts and then we'll --but that issue has been brought up. Okay. All right. Did you want to go first, sir?

PLAINTIFF D. BEZAIRE: Yes, Your Honor.

THE COURT: Okay. All right. Go ahead.

PLAINTIFF D. BEZAIRE: The, the basis of our claim is that we feel that PayPal was negligent in servicing our account, which resulted in a financial loss to us. And the reason that we believe that is we, we sold coins on Ebay and the coins were paid for and we verified that the money was in our PayPal account and so we shipped the coins. The next day we got an e-mail from PayPal saying that the payment was potentially made fraudulently.

We tried to stop shipment of the package. We went to our local post office first and they said that the package had already made it to Canada, so we contacted Canada Post and Canada Post said --initially they said they would stop the package but then they called back and said that the only way that they could stop the package is by request from law enforcement. And we --so then we called PayPal and requested that they contact law enforcement to stop the package and they refused. And we were not qualified to stop the package since we had no information on the fraud and when we asked PayPal for information on the potential fraud they declined to give us any.

So the package was delivered and we no longer had our coins and then PayPal determined, apparently, that the payment was made fraudulently and took the money out of our account. So --

THE COURT: And the total amount was how much?

PLAINTIFF D. BEZAIRE: I believe fourteen hundred and thirty-four dollars ($1,434) .

THE COURT: Okay. All right. Now, the coins were your coins?

PLAINTIFF H. BEZAIRE: Yes, sir.

THE COURT: You owned those solely and separately?

PLAINTIFF H. BEZAIRE: Well yes, I inherited them --

THE COURT: Okay.

PLAINTIFF H. BEZAIRE: --from my father.

THE COURT: Okay. All right. Anything you'd like to add?

PLAINTIFF H. BEZAIRE: Well the story is exactly as how I would tell it. I guess I would add that I feel that there was a window of opportunity to prevent all of this from happening, at least from us losing our, our coins. We had identified where the coins were; we asked for PayPal's help. And as advertised on their website at least three times, and we have copies of that as well, they offer and advertise that they work closely with law enforcement all over the world in preventing and stopping fraud as it's happening. And --

THE COURT: Okay. If you want to get those documents together I'll --

(Plaintiff's confer.)

THE COURT: Or do you have a, a --

PLAINTIFF H. BEZAIRE: We have a --

THE COURT: --other exhibits?

PLAINTIFF D. BEZAIRE: Yeah, we have all our exhibits --

THE COURT: Okay. Well why don't, why don't you give all the exhibits to the bailiff please.

PLAINTIFF H. BEZAIRE: Right. And that would be –

(Plaintiff Confer)

PLAINTIFF H. BEZAIRE: Yeah. Section, Section 6 in that binder --

THE COURT: Um-hum.

PLAINTIFF H. BEZAIRE: --addresses --and at least three portions are areas on the PayPal website where it has advertised they work closely with law enforcement to stop fraud, stop crime in its tracks. And they give examples of responding immediately and reimbursing funds where found -- that fraud occurred. And so based on that information, if the window of opportunity to stop that package and PayPal's saying quote, "we don't do that", when we asked them for help, we feel that we are owed the funds that, that we are requesting.

And to tell you the truth, if they had at least tried to stop the package, worked with Canada Post to alert the -- the law enforcement there, we might not be here today. At least they would have tried to help us stop this thing in the middle of it occurring.

THE COURT: All right. Anything else?

PLAINTIFF D. BEZAIRE: No, Your Honor.

THE COURT: Okay. Now, what would you like to say on behalf of PayPal?

MS. SQUIRES: This is an unfortunate event. They have lost both their money and the merchandise, but our contention is that it could have been avoided. We warned them before the transaction even took place that it was a risky venture on --

THE COURT: That it was a what?

MS. SQUIRES: A risky transaction.

THE COURT: Um-hum.

MS. SQUIRES: And they chose to ignore our warnings and our guidelines. And they --

THE COURT: Okay. How was, how was that warning given?

MS. SQUIRES: Well what happened was they sold these coins to an account under the name of Lucille Ent (phonetic) in Indiana, and then they sent the coins to a Paul Hewitt {phonetic} in Canada. And two days later PayPal detected that there was an unauthorized credit card use and we notified the Bezaire's of this possible fraudulent transaction and we said, you know, we'll reverse it if you qualify for the reversal protection under our seller protection policy. Our seller protection policy affords up to five thousand dollars {$5,000} per year coverage for unauthorized credit card accounts provided --unauthorized credit card use provided the seller follows our guidelines, and they did not. Actually I have some exhibits right here for you.

THE COURT: All right. If you want to hand those to the bailiff.

MS. SQUIRES: Exhibit C is our seller protection policy. And again, this was --developed to protect sellers from unauthorized credit card use provided they follow, they- selling practices. We had to complete the reversal of the payment because they didn't qualify. Exhibit D is the transaction details page, and this was provided to them before the transaction even took place and it shows that a --seller protection policy ineligible. They could have seen that ahead of even accepting the payment and they could have refused the payment or refunded the payment and not shipped the merchandise. Instead, they shipped the merchandise to a person with a different gender in a different country than the confirmed address that we provided to them. That should have been a red flag. I know what happened. They got caught up in an e-mail that this buyer sent to them giving them some cockamamie story that he couldn't use his PayPal account so he had his secretary pay for it with her account. Well that should have been a red flag. You have to ship to a confirmed address.

If they had sent the item to a confirmed address and it was a false credit card use, the person would have said I didn't buy this, I didn't pay for this, and they would have sent it back and contacted PayPal. We know that, that's why we say you have to use a confirmed address. Instead, they were trusting and that's unfortunate and they sent it to this Canadian address and, you know, the result would have been the same. We caught it two days after the payment. We do have superior fraud protection. But the result would have been the same because when Ms. Ent got her credit card bill eventually, a month later, she would have seen this PayPal charge and she wouldn't have known what it was and she would have filed a charge back.

So that's why we say, our Exhibit F, which is the payment policy, if you --if a transaction is reversed for any reason whatsoever and you don't qualify for seller protection policy, you will owe PayPal the amount of the transaction plus any associated fees. So they had to follow certain requirements and these requirements were based on risk management --principles. They weren't arbitrary. If they had followed them their risk of reversal would have been reduced, but they ignored them so they put themselves at risk. And we gave them all this information before the payment was even accepted, they ignored it. And it's basically like I was saying this check might bounce, so I think that it's not fair to be going after PayPal. We can't be held for their negligence when we've given them all the tools to protect themselves. They would be going after this Paul Hewitt in Canada, he has the merchandise.

THE COURT: Well sometimes that's difficult even to sue somebody from out of the State of California. Okay. Now, anything further by either of you?

PLAINTIFF D. BEZAIRE: Yes, Your Honor. You know, whether the transaction was risky or not risky is really a moot point. The bottom line is when we had an opportunity to stop the shipment from occurring all we needed was some slight assistance that they advertise they do everyday on their website and they refused. And that, that refusal directly resulted in our financial loss.

THE COURT: All right. Okay. I'm going to take everything under submission --

MS. SQUIRES: Excuse me, may I address that?

THE COURT: Yes, um-hum.

MS. SQUIRES: We will work with law enforcement as we advertise, but plaintiffs have to contact law enforcement and then law enforcement contacts us. We don't work with them directly because we gave them all the information they needed ahead of time. We work with law enforcement after the fact when we know that there's some kind of criminal disputing going on or some investigation.

THE COURT: I'll take the case under submission and I'll allow both sides to submit any further information or cases regarding the venue 'cause we haven't passed the venue at this point. I'm going to do some independent research but if there's other information you want to send that's fine, please send a copy to them. If you send other information, please -- send a copy to them. Now, how long would you like to submit that?

PLAINTIFF D. BEZAIRE: A month? Would a month –

THE COURT: I can, I can go a month. This is an unusual case. Today's the 6th, so how about by April 7th? And that would be by 9:00 a.m. here to Division 1. And you can send it directly to my attention. So April 7th, 9:00 a.m., 12 Division 1. And everything is under submission.

MS. SQUIRES: Your Honor, I want to be sure that you have the orders for both Orange County --

THE COURT: I, I, I have reviewed some of those.

MS. SQUIRES: Including Compton. So if you need copies I have them here.

THE COURT: Well, but you know, a lot, a lot of case turn on their individual facts and there is the case that was submitted, I don't know if the <u>Combs</u> case was submitted at the other jurisdictions. I don't know the dates and times, so I'm, I'm trying to give everybody an opportunity to submit everything that you'd like. All right. Well thank you. Then please submit anything else you'd like by that date.

PROCEEDINGS CONCLUDED

* * * * *

PayPal Trick #7

If All Else Fails, Try Deceiving the Court

The certified transcript of the trial shows that PayPal, through their representative Michelle Squires, states, "This Comb case is currently on appeal in the 9th Circuit and we believe it's going to be reversed." The Court later says that "it's been submitted that the Comb case is currently on appeal." The Court, relying on PayPal's representation says, "I'm not saying it's going to get reversed but there's a possibility that the case could be reversed." There is no doubt in my mind that PayPal was again trying to perform another smoke and mirror trick trying to make this case disappear. PayPal knew, or should have known, the appeal was dismissed by stipulation, over one year ago in 2005. A copy of that stipulation is shown on the next page. Also see the Declaration of Robert A. Pool starting on p. 85, indicating that <u>Comb</u> has been cited in many jurisdictions and is still applicable. This Declaration was submitted to the Court on March 15, 2006 to show the court the case was NOT on appeal as stated by PayPal.

DOCKETED

ORIGINAL

FILED

JAN 2 6 2005

CATHY A. CATTERSON, CLERK
U.S. COURT OF APPEALS

UNITED STATES COURT OF APPEALS

FOR THE NINTH CIRCUIT

MARK FAWCETT, on behalf of himself and all other similarly situated and on behalf of the general public of the United States; et al.,	No. 02-16876, 02-16879
	D.C. No. CV-02-01227-JF Northern District of California, San Jose
Plaintiffs - Appellees,	
v.	
	ORDER
PAYPAL, INC., a Delaware corporation,	
Defendant - Appellant.	

The stipulation to dismiss the appeal under Federal Rules of Appellate

Procedure 42(b) without prejudice to reinstatement is granted. The costs shall be

allocated pursuant to the stipulation. A certified copy of this order shall act as and

for the mandate of this court. The motion to reinstate is due 28 days after the day

settlement does not become final as stated in the stipulation.

For the Court:

CATHY A. CATTERSON
Clerk of the Court

Grace S. Santos
Deputy Clerk
Ninth Circuit Rule 27-7/Advisory Note to Rule 27
and Ninth Circuit 27-10

Pro 1.24

Declaration of Robert A. Pool

ROBERT A. POOL declares as follows:

I make this declaration on personal knowledge of the facts herein set forth, and am competent and willing to give further testimony if so requested.

I am an active member of the California State Bar, admitted to practice in all courts of the State of California. I am also a member of the Federal District Court for the Central District of California.

I am a member of the law firm Gangloff, Gangloff & Pool, with offices located at 16600 Woodruff Avenue, Suite 215, Bellflower, California.

As *a pro bona publico* service, I recently undertook the request of David Bezaire and Heidi Bezaire to determine whether the case, *Comb v. PayPal, Inc.,* 218 F.Supp.2d 1165 (2002) *("Comb")* has been challenged on appeal in the United States Court of Appeals for the Ninth Circuit, since the Federal District Court for the Northern District of California, San Jose Division, filed its decision in *Comb* on August 30, 2002.

I utilized the proprietary on-line legal research service, LEXIS, to which my law firm subscribes, to conduct research about the *Comb* federal district court case. LEXIS readily located the *Comb* case upon my initial inquiry, using the search term "PayPal." I mark as Exhibit "1," attach to this Declaration, and incorporate the same Exhibit as though here set forth at length, a true copy of the *Comb* decision, as delivered by LEXIS.

Once I located the *Comb* decision in LEXIS, I next employed LEXIS' Shepard's citation service on-line. Attorneys and courts routinely use a cross-referencing process, commonly referred to as "Shepardizing," to accurately determine whether a given case has been affected by subsequent judicial action. I mark as Exhibit "2," attach to this Declaration, and incorporate the same Exhibit as though here set forth at length, a true copy of the LEXIS shepardized report on the *Comb* opinion.

When I examined the document set forth in Exhibit "2" of this Declaration, I first noted that at the top of each page of the five-page Shepard's report appears the summary, "51 citing references" to *Comb*. The five individual pages in Exhibit "2" contain the 51 citing references in detail, arranged numerically 1 through 51, with short summaries that identifies the type of citation, and the source of that particular citation, whether a court, statute annotation, law review and article, legal encyclopedia, or legal treatise.

I next noted that on the first page of the Shepard's report in Exhibit "2" there has been "no subsequent appellate history," of *Comb*. As a California attorney admitted to practice law before all California State Courts, and before the United States District Court for the Central District of California, 1 understand this particular description to mean that there is no pending appellate review in the United States Court of Appeals for the Ninth Circuit, nor in the United States Supreme Court, the only federal courts in which the *Comb* decision might be reviewed.

Based on my personal familiarity with the Shepard's feature *of LEXIS, I* know that when a case has been appealed to a higher court, as might occur, for example, when a decision by a U.S. District Court is challenged in the U.S. Court of Appeals of a given Circuit, or in the U.S. Supreme Court, the Shepard's report will provide *a* bold text, color-coded alert that such an event has taken place. Shepard's on-line feature in LEXIS uses the three colors of a traffic signal --green, yellow, or red - to represent the visual alert on a given case's status. Although in the printed version of the Shepard's report in Exhibit "2" the color signal does not display (Rather, Exhibit "2" states on page one of the Shepard's report, *"SHEPARD'S Signal: Positive treatment is indicated," (Bolded,* italicized emphasis in original).), the same Shepard's report viewed on-line includes a green diamond as an added visual alert of the favorable case status of *Comb*. To confittii my understanding of the Shepard's visual alert system and coding, I compared another case with which I am familiar, *General Motors Corporation v. Franchise Tax Bd.* (2004) 120 Cal.App.4th 114. I already knew that the California Supreme Court has granted review of the Court of Appeal decision in the *General*

Motors case. When I searched for the *General Motors* case in LEXIS, as I anticipated, the Shepard's Signal displayed a red octagon, shaped like a traffic stop sign, and boldly announced that the case was in process of being reviewed by California's highest court, and warning that one should not rely on the opinion filed by the California Court of Appeal in that case.

I further noted that the Shepard's report in Exhibit "2" that *Comb* has been "followed" in two subsequent federal courts. As a California attorney admitted to practice law before all California State Courts, and before the United States District Court for the Central District of California, I understand that when one case is "followed" by a later case, it means the later court approved the legal reasoning employed in the earlier decision. Thus, the two cases that "followed" *Comb* relied on the legal reasoning of the *Comb* decision. The two cases that followed *Comb* both were federal district courts: One, in 2003, the U.S. District Court for the Northern District of Ohio, located within the jurisdiction of the Sixth Circuit of the U.S. Court of Appeals; the other, also in 2003, the U.S. District Court for the Northern District of California, which is the same federal court that originally decided *Comb,* and that falls within the jurisdiction of the Ninth Circuit of the U.S. Court of Appeals, as does *Comb* itself.

The Shepard's report in Exhibit "2" also discloses that *Comb* has been "cited" by federal and state courts in other later decisions on five distinct occasions. As a California attorney admitted to practice law before all California State Courts, and before the United States District Court for the Central District of California, I understand that when a case is "cited" by a later case, it usually means that the later court decision is relying on the undisturbed authoritative statement of a given legal principle that is discussed in the cited case. In 2004, the U.S. District Court for the District of Kansas cited *Comb.* That same year the California Court of Appeal in an unpublished opinion cited *Comb,* as did the Rhode Island Superior Court. In 2005, the U.S. District Court for the Northern District of California also cited *Comb.*

Subsequent citations to *Comb* by federal and state courts, without any reference that *Comb* has been altered by subsequent judicial action, strongly suggest that *Comb* retains its legitimacy and vitality as an undisturbed judicial determination by the U.S. District Court.

LEXIS maintains a proprietary annotated United States Code, known as the United States Code Service (U.S.C.S.). LEXIS' U.S.C.S. includes a citation to *Comb* in that Service's version of Title 9, section 2 of the United States Code. I personally reviewed that annotation, and determined that no indication is there given that *Comb* has been reversed, modified, or disapproved by any subsequent judicial action after the case became final. The absence of such information is consistent with the Shepard's report in Exhibit "2" that there is "no subsequent appellate history" concerning *Comb*. Section 2 of Title 9, United States Code, is a federal statute concerning whether or not an arbitration agreement in a contract is legally enforceable. The *Comb* decision is referenced under that section and title of U.S.C.S. as an example of an unenforceable arbitration agreement in a contract. See item 8, page 2 of Exhibit "2."

34 law reviews and legal periodicals are listed in the Shepard's report in Exhibit "2" that cite *Comb*. See items 9 through 42, pages 2 through 5 of Exhibit "2." I did not attempt to read each of those 34 publications, but I did note that of the sources are by prestigious academic law schools across the nation, including Harvard Law Review, New York University Law Review, and Chicago University Law Review.

The encyclopedic *American Law Reports (A.L.R.)* is an important legal research tool that attorneys and courts rely on for up-to-date national jurisprudential information on all aspects of American law. *Comb* is cited in volume 106 of the 5th series A.L.R., per the Shepard's report, page 5 of Exhibit

Eight legal treatise citations to *Comb* under the headings of computer contracts, computer law, consumer credit law, debtor-creditor law, and internet law also appear in the Shepard's report on page 5 of Exhibit "2."

1 declare under penalty of perjury under the laws of the State of California that the foregoing is true and correct.

Executed at Bellflower, California on March 10, 2006.

Robert A. Pool

*****

I now leave it up to you to make up your own mind of whether the Comb case was on appeal when PayPal said it was during the hearing.

For the sake of brevity, Exhibit 2 is omitted. I will email that to any judicial officer if they send an email to Paul@Rebel101.com asking for it. Please indicate your judicial position.

Appendix B
Frequently Asked Questions

Q. Do you know if my lawsuit has to be filed in San Jose, CA? I live in Illinois. Just talked with my local courthouse and it's not a registered business of Illinois. Some other clerk there at the California courthouse says I have to file it there. It's not cost effective or reasonable for me to travel and litigate this for $1400 in damages.

A. Your business was conducted via your computer in ILL. As far as I know, most jurisdictions permit a complaint to be filed in the jurisdiction where the transaction took place. Call JIM SHEA at JIM SHEA INVESTIGATIONS 2924 David Avenue, San Jose, CA 95128, 408-205-0548. He will serve the Summons and Complaint for you. He will also tell you he serves out-of-California Summons and Complaints all the time.

Q. What do I need to do to file a complaint?

A. Go to your local courthouse and tell them you want to file a small claims complaint. It might be as short as one page or as many as three pages. Pay the filing fee and then have JIM SHEA INVESTIGATIONS 2924 David Avenue, San Jose, CA 95128 408-205-0548 serve it on the defendant.

Q. Do I need to tell everything in my complaint?

A. Just say something like: "Defendant is holding money that belongs to me" or "Defendant took my money and refuses to return it to me." But that all depends on your local jurisdiction. Ask the clerk to help you.

Q. The clerk said I need to file my complaint in California.

A. Ask to speak to the senior clerk. Read the answer to the top question on this list.

Q. Can I sue for punitive damages?

A. Ask for all you can. I hope that judges will begin awarding punitive damages when they see how defendants are being less that fully honest with them. Ask the judge if he would like to see a copy of this book. You might even print a copy and leave it with him.

Q. I use PayPal so people can charge stuff with me. Is there another way for me to go so I can accept payment?

A. Yes there is. Visit http://www.995merchantaccounts.com. You can have an account in a very short time. I refuse to order from any vendor that only uses PayPal for payment.

Q. Can I sue in a foreign country?

A. I am not familiar with all foreign laws. If I was in a foreign country I would file and see what happens. What do you have to lose? The business was conducted from your computer, so don't let a clerk tell you that you must file in California. Ask to speak to a senior clerk and show them the material from my book. Please let me know what happens.

Q. How quickly does PayPal pay after a judgment is issued against them?

A. I didn't even have to send a demand letter, they paid right away – within five days. David, the plaintiff in Case #2, said, "PayPal paid me. I didn't even have to send them something in writing. I was going to wait until the end of the appeal period, then send them something. But a few days after i got the ruling from the court, I got a letter from PayPal saying they would pay me. A few days later, I got a check. I guess they know when they have been beat."

Appendix C

The Court Grants Motion for Change of Venue and Dismisses Without Prejudice

In Case #2, PayPal submitted the following cases to the court showing how other courts have ruled in their favor. Those cases are referred to on page 28. Thank God, David had a judge who was not fooled by their fourth trick as shown on pages 27 to 35. On page 82, the court tells Paypal, "Well, but you know, a lot, a lot of the cases turn on their individual facts and there is the case that was submitted, I don't know if the Combs case was submitted in other jurisdictions."

The following pages show the actual documents from other cases PayPal submitted in an attempt to make their case disappear. Note that every case was dismissed without prejudice, meaning the plaintiff can re-file again. You can now see how important it is for you to bring the Combs case to the attention of the court.

SUPERIOR COURT OF CALIFORNIA, COUNTY OF LOS ANGELES
WEST DISTRICT, CULVER COURTHOUSE, (19437)
4130 OVERLAND AVENUE, CULVER CITY, CA 90231
TELEPHONE: (310) 202-3163

ELLZEY, MAX   vs.
EBAY, INC.   CASE NUMBER: CC 04B01932

MINUTE ORDER and CLERK'S NOTICE OF RULING

Court convened at 01:30 PM, on 12/06/2004; in Division 003

Present: Honorable RALPH AMADO COMMISSIONER, Judge/Comm. Presiding.
         L. CAIN , Deputy Clerk;
and the following proceedings were had:

PLAINTIFF(S) ELLZEY, MAX Appearing.
DEFENDANT(S) EBAY, INC.   (NOT) Appearing.

NATURE OF PROCEEDINGS: CAUSE CALLED FOR HEARING RE: CHALLENGE TO VENUE:

DISPOSITION:
THE COURT RULES THAT THE VENUE IS IMPROPER IN THIS CASE AND
ORDERS THE CASE DISMISSED WITHOUT PREJUDICE PER SECTION C.C.P. 116.370.

The foregoing minutes are correct.   L. CAIN
                                                 Deputy Clerk

---

CLERK'S CERTIFICATE OF MAILING/NOTICE OF ENTRY OF ORDER

I, the below named Executive Officer/Clerk of the above-entitled court, do hereby
certify that I am not a party to the cause herein, and that this date I served
Minute Order/Notice of Ruling the above minute order of
12/06/2004 upon each party or counsel named below by depositing in the
United States mail at the courthouse in CULVER CITY, CALIFORNIA,
one copy of the original entered herein in a separate sealed envelope for each,
addressed as shown below with the postage thereon fully prepaid.

ELLZEY, MAX   EBAY, INC.
                                          AGENT FOR SERVICE-NATIONAL REGISTERED
4183 VINTON AVE.   2030 MAIN STREET, SUITE 1030
CULVER CITY, CA 90232   IRVINE, CA 92614

                    JOHN A. CLARKE, Executive Officer/Clerk

Dated: 12/06/2004   by: L. CAIN Deputy

```
                SUPERIOR COURT OF CALIFORNIA, COUNTY OF LOS ANGELES
                WEST DISTRICT, SANTA MONICA COURTHOUSE, (19484)
                1725 MAIN STREET, SANTA MONICA, CA 90401
                        TELEPHONE: (310) 587-2442

SERAFINER, FRANK              vs.
EBAY, INC                                     CASE NUMBER: SM  04A01253

              MINUTE ORDER and CLERK'S NOTICE OF RULING

Court convened at  09:00 AM, on 08/12/2004; in Department WET

Present:Honorable ROBERTA H. KYMAN, Judge/Comm. Presiding.
        GAIL E. BLOCK , Deputy Clerk;
and the following proceedings were had:

PLAINTIFF(S) SERAFINER, FRANK (NOT) Appearing.
DEFENDANT(S) EBAY, INC (NOT) Appearing.

NATURE OF PROCEEDINGS: CAUSE CALLED FOR HEARING RE: CHALLENGE TO VENUE:


DISPOSITION:
THE COURT RULES THAT THE VENUE IS IMPROPER IN THIS CASE AND
ORDERS THE CASE DISMISSED WITHOUT PREJUDICE PER SECTION C.C.P. 116.370.
```

```
The foregoing minutes are correct.              GAIL E. BLOCK
                                                Deputy Clerk
```
───
```
         CLERK'S CERTIFICATE OF MAILING/NOTICE OF ENTRY OF ORDER

   I, the below named Executive Officer/Clerk of the above-entitled court, do hereby
   certify that I am not a party to the cause herein, and that this date I served
   Minute Order/Notice of Ruling the above minute order of
   08/12/2004 upon each party or counsel named below by depositing in the
   United States mail at the courthouse in SANTA MONICA, CALIFORNIA,
   one copy of the original entered herein in a separate sealed envelope for each,
   addressed as shown below with the postage thereon fully prepaid.
```
───
```
   SERAFINER, FRANK                          EBAY, INC
                                             C/O GLOBAL ACCOUNTING GROUP
   23319 BOCANA STREET                       2145 HAMILTON AVENUE
   MALIBU, CA 90265                          SAN JOSE, CA 95125




                        JOHN A. CLARKE, Executive Officer/Clerk

Dated 08/12/2004             By GAIL E. BLOCK, Deputy
```

SUPERIOR COURT OF CALIFORNI. COUNTY OF ORANGE   SC-130
Harbor Justice Center - Newport Beach Facility
4601 Jamboree Road
Newport Beach, CA 92660-2595   SMALL CLAIMS CASE NO.   05HS01290

NOTICE TO ALL PLAINTIFFS AND DEFENDANTS:	AVISO A TODOS LOS DEMANDANTES Y DEMANDADOS:
Your small claims case has been decided. If you lost the case, and the court ordered you to pay money, your wages, money, and property may be taken without further warning from the court. Read the back of this sheet for important information about your rights.	Su caso ha sido resuelto por la corte para reclamos judiciales menores. Si la corte ha decidido en su contra y ha ordenado que usted pague dinero, le pueden quitar su salario, su dinero, y otras cosas de su propiedad, sin aviso adicional por parte de esta corte. Lea el reverso de este formulario para obtener información de importancia acerca de sus derechos.

PLAINTIFF/DEMANDANTE *(Name, street address and telephone number of each)*
GOREN, OFER A.
329 DAHLIA PLACE
CORONA DEL MAR, CA 92625

Telephone No.

PLAINTIFF/DEMANDANTE *(Name, street address and telephone number of each)*

Telephone No.

DEFENDANT/DEMANDADO *(Name, street address and telephone number of each)*
PAY PAL INC., A CA CORP.
2145 HAMILTON AVE.
SAN JOSE, CA 95125

Telephone No.

DEFENDANT/DEMANDADO *(Name, street address, and telephone number of each)*

Telephone No.

☐ See attached sheet for additional plaintiffs and defendants.

NOTICE OF ENTRY OF JUDGMENT

Judgment was entered as checked below on *(date):*   AUG 0 5 2005   H. WARREN SIEGEL

1. ☐ Defendant *(name, if more than one):*
shall pay plaintiff *(name, if more than one):*
$ principal and: $ costs on plaintiff's claim.
2. ☐ Defendant does not owe plaintiff any money on plaintiff's claim.
3. ☐ Plaintiff *(name, if more than one):*
shall pay defendant *(name, if more than one):*
$ principal and : $ costs on defendant's claim.
4. ☐ Plaintiff does not owe defendant any money on defendant's claim.
5. ☐ Possession of the following property is awarded to plaintiff *(describe property):*

6. ☐ Payments are to be made at the rate of: $ per *(specify period):*   , beginning on *(date):*
and on the *(specify day):*   day of each month thereafter until paid in full. If any payment is missed, the entire balance may become due immediately.
7. ☒ Dismissed in court ☐ with prejudice ☒ without prejudice.
8. ☐ Attorney-Client Fee Dispute (Attachment to Notice of Entry of Judgment) (form SC-132) is attached.
9. ☒ Other *(specify):* Change of Venue granted.

10. ☐ This judgment results from a motor vehicle accident on a California highway and was caused by the judgment debtor's operation of a motor vehicle. If the judgment is not paid, the judgment creditor may apply to have the judgment debtor's driver's license suspended.
11. Enforcement of the judgment is automatically postponed for 30 days or, if an appeal is filed, until the appeal is decided.
12. ☐ This notice was personally delivered to *(insert name and date).*
13. CLERK'S CERTIFICATE OF MAILING—I certify that I am not a party to this action. This *Notice of Entry of Judgment* was mailed first class, postage prepaid, in a sealed envelope to the parties at the addresses shown above. The mailing and this certification occurred at the place and on the date shown below.
Place of mailing: Newport Beach, California

Date of mailing: AUG 0 5 2005   Alan Slater, Clerk, by   , Deputy

—The county provides small claims advisor services free of charge. Read the information sheet on the reverse.—

Form Adopted for Mandatory Use
Judicial Council of California
SC-130 [Rev. January 1, 2000]
F0084-2994 [R11/03]

NOTICE OF ENTRY OF JUDGMENT
(Small Claims)

Cal. Rules of Court, rule 982.7
Code of Civil Procedure §116.610

—NOTICE TO ALL PLAINTIFFS AND DEFENDANTS—

SC-130

SUPERIOR COURT OF CALIFORNIA. COUNTY OF ORANGE
NORTH JUSTICE CENTER
1275 North Berkeley Ave.
P.O. Box 5000
Fullerton, CA 92838-0500

SMALL CLAIMS CASE NO.: 04NS76770

NOTICE TO ALL PLAINTIFFS AND DEFENDANTS: Your small claims case has been decided. If you lost the case, and the court ordered you to pay money, your wages, money, and property may be taken without further warning from the court. Read the back of this sheet for important information about your rights.	AVISO A TODOS LOS DEMANDANTES Y DEMANDADOS: Su caso ha sido resuelto por la corte para reclamos judiciales menores. Si la corte ha decidido en su contra y ha ordenado que usted pague dinero, le pueden quitar su salario, su dinero, y otras cosas de su propiedad, sin aviso adicional por parte de esta corte. Lea el reverso de este formulario para obtener información de importancia acerca de sus derechos.

PLAINTIFF/DEMANDANTE (Name, street address, and telephone number of each):

TSE, RICK K.
2600 W. LA HABRA BL. #228
LA HABRA, CA 90631

Telephone No.: 626-810-1082

DEFENDANT/DEMANDADO (Name, street address, and telephone number of each):

PAYPAL AN EBAY COMPANY
2211 N. FIRST ST.
SAN JOSE, CA 95131

Telephone No.:

Telephone No.:

Telephone No.:

[ ] See attached sheet for additional plaintiffs and defendants.

NOTICE OF ENTRY OF JUDGMENT

Judgment was entered as checked below on (date): 03/02/2005

1. [ ] Defendant (name, if more than one):
   shall pay plaintiff (name, if more than one):
   $ principal and: $ costs on plaintiff's claim.
2. [ ] Defendant does not owe plaintiff any money on plaintiff's claim.
3. [ ] Plaintiff (name, if more than one):
   shall pay defendant (name, if more than one).
   $ principal and: $ costs on defendant's claim.
4. [ ] Plaintiff does not owe defendant any money on defendant's claim.
5. [ ] Possession of the following property is awarded to plaintiff (describe property):

6. [ ] Payments are to be made at the rate of: $ per (specify period): , beginning on (date):
   and on the (specify day): day of each month thereafter until paid in full. If any payment is missed, the entire balance may become due immediately.
7. [xx] Dismissed in court [ ] with prejudice [xx] without prejudice.
8. [xx] Attorney-Client Fee Dispute (Attachment to Notice of Entry of Judgment) (form SC-132) is attached.
9. [xx] Other (specify):
   CHALLENGE OF VENUE GRANTED. DEFENDANT'S NOT PRESENT

10. [ ] This judgment results from a motor vehicle accident on a California highway and was caused by the judgment debtor's operation of a motor vehicle. If the judgment is not paid, the judgment creditor may apply to have the judgment debtor's driver's license suspended.
11. Enforcement of the judgment is automatically postponed for 30 days or, if an appeal is filed, until the appeal is decided.
12. [ ] This notice was personally delivered to (insert name and date):
13. CLERK'S CERTIFICATE OF MAILING—I certify that I am not a party to this action. This Notice of Entry of Judgment was mailed first class, postage prepaid, in a sealed envelope to the parties at the addresses shown above. The mailing and this certification occurred at the place and on the date shown below.

Place of mailing: FULLERTON , California

Date of mailing: 04/18/2005 ALAN SLATER Clerk, by KATHY CRITSER , Deputy

The county provides small claims advisor services free of charge. Read the information sheet on the reverse.

NOTICE OF ENTRY OF JUDGMENT
(Small Claims)

Minute Orders

Home	Complaints/Parties	Actions	Minutes
Pending Hearings	Images	Case Report	

Action: (Choose)

SMALL CLAIMS HEARING
01/15/2004 - 8:30 AM DEPT. 12

PAULETTE DURAND-BARKLEY PRESIDING.
CLERK: A. FLICKINGER
REPORTER: NONE
NO APPEARANCE BY: SAMUEL L. DAVIS, PAYPAL, INC.
COURT HAS READ AND CONSIDERED DEFENDANTS MOTION CHALLENGING VENUE IN THIS ACTION.
MOTION BY DEFENDANT RE CHALLENGE TO VENUE IS CALLED FOR HEARING.
MOTION GRANTED
ENTIRE ACTION DISMISSED PLAINTIFF'S CLAIM OF SAMUEL DAVIS
NOTICE SENT TO SAMUEL L. DAVIS
NOTICE SENT TO PAYPAL, INC.

SUPERIOR COURT OF CALIFORNIA, COUNTY OF LOS ANGELES
SOUTHEAST DISTRICT, HUNTINGTON PARK COURTHOUSE, (-19480-)
6548 MILES AVENUE, HUNTINGTON PK, CA 90255-0609
TELEPHONE: (323) 586-6359

VIA TRADING CORPORATION   vs.
EBAY INC.   CASE NUMBER: HP 05S01674

MINUTE ORDER and CLERK'S NOTICE OF RULING

Court convened at 01:30 PM, on 08/15/2005; in Division 002

Present:Honorable REGINALD A. DUNN, Judge/Comm. Presiding.
         R.SANCHEZ , Deputy Clerk;
and the following proceedings were had:

PLAINTIFF(S) VIA TRADING CORPORATION Appearing.
DEFENDANT(S) EBAY INC. (NOT) Appearing.

NATURE OF PROCEEDINGS: CAUSE CALLED FOR SMALL CLAIMS HEARING:

DISPOSITION:
NO APPEARANCE BY FOR DEFENDANT(S). THE COURT ORDERS CASE
DISMISSED WITHOUT PREJUDICE.
(COURT HAS READ AND CONSIDERED DEFENDANT`S LETTER.COURT
DETERMINES VENUE IS IMPROPER.)
CLERK TO SEND NOTICE OF RULING.

The foregoing minutes are correct.   R.SANCHEZ
                                           Deputy Clerk

CLERK'S CERTIFICATE OF MAILING/NOTICE OF ENTRY OF ORDER

    I, the below named Executive Officer/Clerk of the above-entitled court, do hereby
certify that I am not a party to the cause herein, and that this date I served
Minute Order/Notice of Ruling the above minute order of
08/15/2005 upon each party or counsel named below by depositing in the
United States mail at the courthouse in HUNTINGTON PK, CALIFORNIA,
one copy of the original entered herein in a separate sealed envelope for each,
addressed as shown below with the postage thereon fully prepaid.

VIA TRADING CORPORATION   EBAY INC.

2100 SATURN AVENUE   2211 NORTH FIRST STREET
HUNTINGTON PAR, CA 90255   SAN JOSE, CA 95131

                    JOHN A. CLARKE, Executive Officer/Clerk

Dated 08/15/2005   By R.SANCHEZ, Deputy

```
              SUPERIOR COURT OF CALIFORNIA, COUNTY OF LOS ANGELES
              SOUTH CENTRAL DISTRICT, COMPTON COURTHOUSE, (-19435-)
              200 WEST COMPTON BLVD., COMPTON, CA 90220
                      TELEPHONE: (310) 603-7842

BACA, DAVID ROBERT            vs.
PAYPAL, INC.                                    CASE NUMBER: COM 05S00713

        MINUTE ORDER and CLERK'S NOTICE OF RULING

  Court convened at  08:30 AM, on 05/18/2005; in Department OOP

  Present: Honorable GARY R. HAHN, Judge/Comm. Presiding.
          S. CROSBY , Deputy Clerk;
  and the following proceedings were had:

  PLAINTIFF(S)  BACA, DAVID ROBERT Appearing.
  DEFENDANT(S)  PAYPAL, INC. - LEGAL DEPARTMENT (NOT) Appearing.

  NATURE OF PROCEEDINGS: CAUSE CALLED


  DISPOSITION:
  COURT ORDERS CASE DISMISSED WITH PREJUDICE.
```

```
The foregoing minutes are correct.        S. CROSBY
                                           Deputy Clerk
```

```
          CLERK'S CERTIFICATE OF MAILING/NOTICE OF ENTRY OF ORDER

  I, the below named Executive Officer/Clerk of the above-entitled court, do hereby
  certify that I am not a party to the cause herein, and that this date I served
  Minute Order/Notice of Ruling the above minute order of
  05/18/2005 upon each party or counsel named below by depositing in the
  United States mail at the courthouse in COMPTON, CALIFORNIA,
  one copy of the original entered herein in a separate sealed envelope for each,
  addressed as shown below with the postage thereon fully prepaid.
```

```
  BACA, DAVID ROBERT                    PAYPAL, INC. - LEGAL DEPARTMENT
                                        C/O  NATIONAL REGISTERED AGENTS, INC.
  18412 TOWNE AVE.                      2030 MAIN ST. #1030
  CARSON, CA 90746                      IRVINE, CA 92614
```

```
                    JOHN A. CLARKE, Executive Officer/Clerk

  Dated 05/18/2005          By S. CROSBY Deputy
```

```
             SUPERIOR COURT OF CALIFORNIA, COUNTY OF LOS ANGELES
             NORTH CENTRAL DISTRICT, BURBANK COURTHOUSE, (-19425-)
             300 E. OLIVE AVENUE, BURBANK, CA 91502
                     TELEPHONE: (818) 557-3461

MOSDALE, BRIAN                        vs.
EBAY, INC.                                          CASE NUMBER: BUR 04S00696

        MINUTE ORDER and CLERK'S NOTICE OF RULING

Court convened at  08:30 AM, on 12/07/2004; in Division 003

Present:Honorable DENNIS L. SHANKLIN, COMMISSIONER, Judge/Comm. Presiding.
        MICHAEL ORTIZ , Deputy Clerk;
and the following proceedings were had:

PLAINTIFF(S) MOSDALE, BRIAN Appearing.
DEFENDANT(S) EBAY, INC., DBA  SQUARE TRADE              NOT Appearing.

NATURE OF PROCEEDINGS: CAUSE CALLED FOR HEARING RE: CHALLENGE TO VENUE:


DISPOSITION:
THE COURT RULES THAT THE VENUE IS IMPROPER IN THIS CASE AND
ORDERS THE CASE DISMISSED WITHOUT PREJUDICE PER SECTION C.C.P. 116.370.
```

```
The foregoing minutes are correct.              MICHAEL ORTIZ
                                                Deputy Clerk

          CLERK'S CERTIFICATE OF MAILING/NOTICE OF ENTRY OF ORDER

·I, the below named Executive Officer/Clerk of the above-entitled court, do hereby
certify that I am not a party to the cause herein, and that this date I served
Minute Order/Notice of Ruling the above minute order of
12/07/2004 upon each party or counsel named below by depositing in the
United States mail at the courthouse in BURBANK, CALIFORNIA,
one copy of the original entered herein in a separate sealed envelope for each,
addressed as shown below with the postage thereon fully prepaid.
```

```
MOSDALE, BRIAN                          EBAY, INC. DBA  SQUARE TRADE
                                        ATTN: BARBARA GOODING
1520 ONTARIO ST                         2145 HAMILTON AVE
BURBANK, CA 91505                       SAN JOSE, CA 95125




                           JOHN A. CLARKE, Executive Officer/Clerk

Dated 12/07/2004           B: MICHAEL ORTIZ  Deputy
```

Cover Design by Develonet.com